MW00986133

TALKS

Motivating
Acquisition-Centered
Classrooms

Eric Herman

Acquisition Classroom

Research Talks:
Motivating Acquisition-Centered Classrooms

Book and Cover Design by Eric Herman
Cover Art by www.bigstock.com

eric.herman.pchn@gmail.com

AC | Acquisition Classroom
www.acquisitionclassroom.weebly.com

ISBN: 9781073118809

Printed in the United States of America

First Edition: 2019

10 9 8 7 6 5 4 3 2 1

For language teachers who have adopted research-supported practices, and for those who want to do so.

About the Author

Eric Herman is a Ph.D. student in Hispanic Linguistics at Florida State University. He obtained his M.A. in Hispanic Linguistics from Florida State University in 2019. He co-teaches an online summer course on second language acquisition and language education as part of a language teacher certificate program at UC Boulder. He

has been a Spanish language teacher at the elementary, middle, university, and adult levels and he taught English in Honduras as part of his service as a Youth Development Volunteer in the Peace Corps. He is the author of the graded reader *Ataques de Hambre* (2016), *Assessing Proficiency in the Classroom* (2017), and the regularly distributed *Acquisition Classroom Memo.*

CONTENTS

Introduction

What is in this book?

The quotes in this book come from articles, papers, and book chapters that have been foundational to the field of second language acquisition (SLA) and that bear major implications for language teaching. They are often cited in the literature and are authored by some of the biggest names in the field. In that sense, the publications are the "classics" of SLA and, just like classics, the quotes express messages that have withstood the test of time. As will become apparent, there are some things that language scientists have known and recommended for a long time.

Each quote is a "one-liner" that delivers the punchline to an important aspect of SLA and/or pedagogical issue. Taken together, these quotes "tell a story" that primarily takes place in the mind/brain of second language learners and of which input is the protagonist. The story spans more than fifty years (and a few quotes date back to the fifteenth-seventeenth centuries). Figure 1 presents the distribution of the works cited, excluding works cited from the earliest educational reformers. The bigger the bar, the more publications cited from that year. There are more than 200 citations, from which most are quoted.

Figure 1. *Timeline of publications cited*

The power of this book is in the numbers, i.e., the findings and ideas are more convincing when similarly expressed by multiple researchers. Many quotes convey "facts" of SLA, i.e., observations of general consensus. There is a lot that even the advocates of different theoretical perspectives agree upon. Sometimes, perspectives on SLA that appear to conflict are actually complementary, because they focus on the development of different types of knowledge or a different aspect of the overall process of language development. When there is potential for competition, the book favors a linguistic perspective, which is one contemporary and mainstream perspective within SLA.

More than three-quarters of the quotes are accompanied by brief commentary, which occasionally include more quotes. Some quotes are self-explanatory and not in need of further comment. For the majority, I provide historical and theoretical context and/or provide more information about a study being cited. A few times, I ask a reflection question or give my interpretation. The comments also contain definitions of key terms from the field of SLA.

I encourage you to read the original sources. The majority of these quotes and comments appeared in Acquisition Classroom Memos, where I summarize and critique foundational works of SLA, as well as discuss the pedagogical implications.

Why this book?

A principal purpose of the book is to educate. The book adopts a "teacher first" approach, i.e., the quotes were selected and ordered and the comments written with a language teacher in mind. It is intended to be a teacher's guide to SLA. The educational system needs teachers who are informed and critical consumers. As Fullan, expert on educational reform, says, "Teacher education still has the honour of being simultaneously the worst problem and the best solution in education. We need desperately to size up the problem, and see what can be done to make the career-long continuum of teacher learning a reality" (1993, p. 105). Fullan is talking about the education of teachers from all subject matters.

However, this book contains quotes about language teacher preparation that "size up the problem," and reveal that there is a serious problem indeed.

What Fullan (1993) calls the "catch 22" is that society "gives teachers failing grades for not producing better results. At the same time, it does not help improve the conditions that would make success possible" (p. 104). In the case of language teaching, consider the amount of SLA education that is part of teacher preparation and teacher development. Fullan goes on to say that teachers also share the responsibility for escaping this catch 22. To that end, this book is for a teacher's self-education, but it also "arms" teachers with the major discoveries and the views of researchers to share with others. I encourage teachers to discuss the quotes with students. One practice I recommend is for teachers to make and hang classroom posters of their favorite quotes. Also, seize the opportunity to be educators outside of the classroom, to share the information with the general public, especially with administrators and parents. If you want to implement research-supported practices, then it may very well be that "paying it [SLA education] forward" is not just beneficial, but necessary. This is especially true when such practices are perceived as "new" and when they conflict with commonly held beliefs about language learning and teaching.

What if beliefs conflict with science?

What I want to make clear is that a (good) scientist's perspective, theories, and hypotheses are not the same thing as beliefs. The difference has to do with what they are based upon. A theory tries to come up with an explanation for multiple findings in SLA and a hypothesis is an explanation for at least one of those findings. Or, as VanPatten and Williams (2015) say, "When we make a prediction based on a theory, we are in effect making a hypothesis" (p. 5). A perspective is more global and encompasses multiple theories, but which all share a common view, e.g., a generative linguistic perspective sees language as abstract properties of the mind that generate sentences and within this perspective there are multiple theories that differ in how they characterize those abstract properties.

Beliefs, on the other hand, are personal and subjective interpretations. They are not based on scientific evidence, such as the results of controlled experimentation, and beliefs may not be testable. Hence why good researchers are not said to "believe" in something. (The bad ones do make claims that are under-supported by the evidence and/or ignore conflicting evidence). Scientists also don't "prove" anything, but rather, find evidence that supports (or doesn't support) something.

When a topic from this book is unfamiliar to the reader, he/she will have the challenging and sometimes uncomfortable task of trying to reconcile beliefs with scientific observations about language, language acquisition, communication, and/or pedagogy. There is a significant gap between SLA and mainstream language teaching, so some readers will undoubtedly experience some dissonance. Rather than commit to a belief, the desired mindset is to commit to the lifelong pursuit of the best answers as to how we acquire languages and how we should teach languages. I hope that this book will motivate future learning, including exposure to alternative ways of teaching. In fact, it is the experience (as a student, observer, and teacher) of a "new" approach that may be the strongest motivator of changes in beliefs.

How is the book organized?

This book can be read straight through or spaced out over time. My recommendation is to read and reflect on one quote per school day, providing you with daily inspiration to align language teaching with language science. The quotes have been organized and ordered for this purpose.

The quotes are divided into weeks. There are five quotes per week (sometimes more), for a total of thirty weeks. Every day of the week contains a quote from a different researcher and is about a different topic (see

Table 1). Although, sometimes the quotes pertain to more than one topic.

Table 1. *Organization of a week*

Day	Topic
Monday	Input, Mental Grammar, Reading, Comprehension
Tuesday	Development, Output, Correction
Wednesday	Textbook Grammar, Dual Systems
Thursday	Communication, Vocabulary, Communicative Tests, Relationships, Enjoyment
Friday	Beliefs, Principles, Education

The topics were ordered this way, because it was considered to be of greatest importance to be reminded the first day of every week about the role of input and the nature of mental grammar. This naturally leaves us wondering, "What about output?" and "What will the development of mental grammar look like?" which is answered by quotes on the following day. The middle of the week, when we are feeling a little tired and perhaps prone to falling back on old teaching behaviors, there are timely quotes about textbook grammar and the distinction between native and non-native language acquisition processes and products. The next day's quotes contrast rule-based instruction with what it means to teach communicatively and present the implications of a communicative approach for other features of program design. The last day invokes us to re-examine our beliefs and proposes guidelines for classroom practice that are based on SLA research. The final day also includes quotes about the current state of language teacher preparation and training, which hopefully encourages more sharing of the quotes and maybe even inspires some over-the-weekend study.

Week 1

INPUT

Comprehension of meaningful language is the foundation of language acquisition.

Lightbown & Spada, 2013, p. 165

DEVELOPMENT

The idea that what you teach is what they learn, and when you teach it is when they learn it, is not just simplistic, it is wrong.

———————

Long, 2000, p. 182

TEXTBOOK GRAMMAR

Beginners in grammar are so overwhelmed by precepts, rules, exceptions to the rules, and exceptions to the exceptions, that for the most part they do not know what they are doing, and are quite stupefied before they begin to understand anything.

———————

Comenius, 1657, p. 196

Comenius (1592-1670) was the most famous educational reformer of the 17th century. He wrote the details of his method in a book titled *Didactica Magna*. He was especially famous for his textbooks, which were based on high-frequency Latin and he wrote the first picture book in the history of education.

COMMUNICATION

The acquisition of other languages through using them for purposes of communication is, on the other hand, as old as language itself... We will refer to this method of acquiring the ability to communicate in another language directly without instruction in its grammar as the traditional approach because the evidence seems clear that in fact this is how most people have traditionally acquired languages.

———

Krashen & Terrell, 1983, p. 7

Terrell first proposed the Natural Approach in 1977, which originally evolved from his teaching experiences. In that 1977 paper, he "suggested three general guidelines which could facilitate L2 acquisition for communicative competence: (1) all classroom activities should be devoted to communication with focus on content, (2) no speech errors should be corrected, and (3) students should feel free to respond in L1, L2 or any mixture of the two" (p. 331-332). Class time was spent on an assortment of interactive activities involving personalized and familiar topics. Terrell teamed up with Krashen in 1983 to write the methods book.

In the early days of SLA, Krashen proposed the Monitor Model (e.g., 1975, 1976, 1977) – perhaps more appropriately considered a model (description) of SLA processes than a theory (explanation) – which consisted of 5 hypotheses and captured some important insights, e.g., the direct role of input, the limits on the effects of rule-based instruction, and the difference between the process and product of comprehending input (i.e., acquisition) versus practicing textbook rules (i.e., learning).

The SLA field today, in general, uses the terms acquisition and learning interchangeably, albeit accepting that comprehending input results in a native type of knowledge and that practicing rules results in a non-native type of knowledge. After all, young children are not learning and practicing rules to acquire their L1 and doing so would engage different mental processes that develop a qualitatively different type of knowledge.

BELIEFS

A good system of education, from this point of view, is not one in which all or most teachers carry out the same recommended classroom procedures but rather a system in which (1) all, or most, teachers operate with a sense of plausibility about whatever procedures they choose to adopt, and (2) each teacher's sense of plausibility is as 'alive' or active, and hence as open to further development or change as it can be.

———

Prabhu, 1987, p. 108

Sense of plausibility is Prabhu's term for a teacher's perception of how learning happens.

Week 2

INPUT

The concept of input is perhaps the single most important concept of second language acquisition. It is trivial to point out that no individual can learn a second language without input of some sort. In fact, no model of second language acquisition does not avail itself of input in trying to explain how learners create second language grammars.

Gass, 2017, p. 1

DEVELOPMENT

Instruction does not appear to influence the order of development. No matter what order grammatical structures are presented and practiced in the classroom, learners will follow their own 'built-in' syllabus.

R. Ellis, 1984, p. 150

TEXTBOOK GRAMMAR

Some structure-based approaches to teaching are based on the false assumption that second language development is an accumulation of rules. This can be seen in the organization of textbooks that introduce a particular language feature in the first unit and reinforce it in several subsequent units, and then move on to the next feature, with only rare opportunities for learners to practice the ones previously taught.

Lightbown & Spada, 2013, p. 207

COMMUNICATION

Viewed from a historical perspective, innovation in second language teaching that is currently labeled 'communicative' is not new in the absolute sense: It is only new to the institutional setting that has repeatedly failed to implement it with its original intent.

Musumeci, 1997, p. 133

BELIEFS

Before any meaningful attempts can be made to implement teaching and testing procedures which reflect what we know about second language learning strategies, however, we have to deal convincingly with the feelings of the classroom teacher. Failure to do so will result in yet another wave of 'reform' consisting of a new set of labels... with nothing really changed.

Savignon, 1976, p. 10

This paper is a must-read classic. Sandra J. Savignon, one of the founders of communicative language teaching, invokes McLuhan's metaphor of the Rearview Mirror Syndrome, which is when new approaches are viewed through an old lens. Despite the warning, what is today labeled "communicative" is most often intended to be a better way to teach a syllabus of word sets and rules and "communicative activities" are treated as an add-on to the old way of doing things. Prior to my own education in SLA, I was also guilty of the syndrome, having written in 2012 in a grammar manual that I was designing for my students, "If the goal is to be able to communicate in Spanish, then it is important to know the general rules for the main parts of speech." However, a communicative (and a proficiency-based) approach is an entirely different system.

11

Week 3

INPUT

Simply put, learners 'get grammar' by attending to comprehensible meaning-bearing input; they don't build a linguistic system up over time as a matter of oral practice.

VanPatten, 1994, p. 28

DEVELOPMENT

The research on developmental sequences makes it clear that progress in a learner's interlanguage will not necessarily show up as greater accuracy. That is, the developmental stages through which learners pass on their way to higher levels of proficiency include stages in which their performance is still far from target-like.

Lightbown, 2000, p. 442

This quote comes from a paper that reaffirms ten generalizations from SLA research, which Lightbown originally published in 1985 under the title "Great Expectations." She argued that SLA research could inform teacher expectations.

In addition to passing through obligatory non-target-like stages, there is also a developmental pattern referred to as "U-shaped," in which a learner's performance actually gets "worse" before it gets better (Kellerman, 1985). For instance, irregular forms are first learned as individual items (e.g., "ate"). Regular past tense endings are later overgeneralized to irregulars ("eated"). Accuracy eventually re-emerges.

13

TEXTBOOK GRAMMAR

In the study of humane letters and the languages there cannot be a set period of time for their completion, because of the difference in abilities and learning of those who hear the lectures, and because of other reasons too.

... all rules of Emmanuel [grammar text] must be divided into three books, of which each is appropriate to a single class... The master practically completes the book of each class during the first semester, and begins from the beginning in the second.

_____

Loyola, 1551, in Ganss, p. 327

_____

Jesuit Society, 1599, in Fitzpatrick, p. 177

Ignatius Loyola (1491-1556) founded the Jesuit Society and developed a new system of education. However, the Jesuit Society's plan for implementing Loyola's ideas deviated substantially from Ignatius's message. Whereas Ignatius advocated the teaching of the humanities in Latin (i.e., immersion schooling) and included theory and practice in his guidelines (i.e., *Constitutions*), the Society left theory out of their manual (i.e., *Ratio Studiorum*). This quote represents what may be the start to the practice of covering a textbook grammar in 3 years. The *Ratio* also describes what would come to be called the "grammar-translation method."

14

COMMUNICATION

This [focus on form, not meaning] may be because language teachers are supposed to teach language and not anything else, just as social studies teachers or science teachers are supposed to teach social studies or science. Though this analogy sounds reasonable enough, the fallacy lies in comparing language, which is 'form,' to subject matter, which is 'content.'

———————

Dulay & Burt, 1973, p. 257

This was stated at the onset of the field of SLA and is still being said today. "Language must be treated differently in the classroom from other subject matters" (VanPatten, 2017, p. 104).

BELIEFS

At a time when so much thoroughly sound theory is available to them, it is a pity that so many foreign language teachers still cling to a few discredited notions of language acquisition. Our foreign language teachers, to say nothing at all about their students, deserve better.

Winitz & Reeds, 1973, p. 295

The authors go on to recommend a comprehension-based, self-study program (i.e., matching pictures to utterances), which would come to be called "The Learnables."

Week 4

INPUT

Conversely, all cases of successful first and second language acquisition are characterized by the availability of comprehensible (not necessarily linguistically modified) input.

Larsen-Freeman & Long, 1991, p. 142

The researchers reviewed the evidence used to support Krashen's input hypothesis and right before this quote, they had discussed what they considered to be "the best evidence for Krashen's viewpoint" (p. 142), which is the lack of acquisition that results when first and second language learners are exposed to incomprehensible input.

OUTPUT

… we are not minimizing the role of comprehension, or input, in SLA theory; rather, we wish to make the case that sometimes, under some conditions, output facilitates second language learning in ways that are different from, or enhance, those of input.

———————

Swain & Lapkin, 1995, p. 371

In 1985, Swain proposed the comprehensible output hypothesis (later just called the output hypothesis), which, by the way, was not based on research on output. It was based on the observation that the grammar of 7-year immersion students was not perfect (e.g., 57% accuracy of verb forms during conversation). But should the students be perfect? Also, what does that 57% figure indicate about developmentally appropriate expectations?

This quote captures how she later qualified her proposal. Swain would again reframe the output hypothesis, this time in sociocultural terms, first proposing the term "collaborative dialogue" (2000) and later "languaging" (2006), which seems to refer to the same thing, i.e., language being used to mediate/shape thought. You say something, reflect on it, and learn from what you said. This can include learners negotiating form (not meaning). In fact, learners are talking *about* language in the studies used to support languaging. More on socioculturalism later.

TEXTBOOK GRAMMAR

No longer the necessary vehicle by which to access interesting subject matter, Latin was reduced at best to a linguistic puzzle or a challenging mental exercise, and at worst to a dull catalogue of abstract, nonsensical rules.

———————

Musumeci, 2009, p. 54

Latin was the medium of instruction in the first universities in the twelfth century, e.g. Oxford. Following medieval times, a new curriculum - the *studia humanitatis* - was proposed. The humanities were to be taught in Latin, i.e., immersion schooling. But in the 16th century, Latin became the object of study, rather than the means of communicating about subject matter.

COMMUNICATION

There is ample evidence that many teachers, but not native speakers or language learners, define effective communication as near perfection in structure and phonology, and thus doom the student to ultimate failure. . . A reappraisal of the goals of foreign language teachers to bring them in line with students' and native speakers' expectations is long overdue.

———————

Terrell, 1977, p. 335

Learner expectations and developmental research conflict with an "accuracy first" approach. In its place, we need a "communication/proficiency first" approach in which accuracy is expected to develop gradually and not on a teacher's or textbook's schedule. Modifying the definition from the American Council on the Teaching of Foreign Languages (ACTFL) (Sandrock, Swender, Cowles, Martin, & Vicars, 2012), I define proficiency as the ability to comprehend and be comprehended across a range of familiar and unfamiliar contexts.

EDUCATION

That only 6% of Spanish faculty and 2% of French faculty have such expertise [in second language acquisition] indicates a major lacuna in [university] 'language' departments. What is more... of the 27 institutions examined, 13 (48%) had no language acquisition experts at all in Spanish, and a whopping 21 (78%) had no language acquisition experts in French. And I remind the reader why I did not include the Ivy League schools: they have 0% language experts across the board...

VanPatten, 2015c, p. 6

A "language acquisition expert" was defined as tenure-line faculty with a PhD in and who conducted research in language science. There has been little change over the past three decades. Teschner (1987) found that only 14% of the language program directors (who are responsible for training graduate teaching assistants) had a PhD in applied or educational linguistics. What are the ramifications for the education of language teachers? What does this all mean for effecting change in language programs?

21

Week 5

INPUT

The language module deals with linguistic information automatically; awareness of input is sufficient for its development...

———————

Truscott & Sharwood Smith, 2011, p. 524

This quote comes from an article that critiques the noticing hypothesis (see also Truscott, 1998). The noticing hypothesis claims that it is necessary and sufficient to consciously detect (but not understand) specific aspects of the input (Schmidt, 1990). The hypothesis has been critiqued on numerous grounds, e.g., vaguely and inconsistently defined, lacks a theory of language and a theory of consciousness, etc. Truscott and Sharwood Smith use their conceptualization of the mind to try to make sense of the noticing hypothesis and conclude that we do not need to consciously notice anything in the input in order to develop the core language system.

Truscott and Sharwood Smith (2004) developed the Modular Cognition Framework, which is an overarching view of the mind that integrates research from linguistics, psychology, and neuroscience. The application of the framework to language and language acquisition is called the Modular Online Growth and Use of Language (MOGUL) Project (Sharwood Smith, 2019). Heavily based on the proposal of a Parallel Architecture by Jackendoff (e.g., 2002), the architecture of first and second languages is proposed to be made up of 3 interconnected modules: phonology (sounds), syntax (word order), and conceptual/semantic structure (meaning). The first two aforementioned modules make up the "language module" or "core language system."

The MOGUL Project argues for Acquisition by Processing Theory, which says that "acquisition is the lingering effects of processing" (2014b, p. 93). Processing input creates new knowledge in a module, connects knowledge between modules, and/or raises the activation level of existing knowledge (output can also do the latter). The higher the activation, the greater the chance of being used during comprehension and production. Growth of the core language system is contrasted with learning metalinguistic knowledge (i.e., information about language).

In many ways, this is an updated and more scientifically rigorous version of Krashen's model. But what we gain in rigor, we lose in readability. In fact, when you read Krashen's work, you wonder whether his intended audience has always included teachers. He wrote in the first chapter of his most-cited book, "There is another goal, however, and that is to reintroduce teachers to theory and hopefully to gain their confidence again" (1982, p. 7-8). And in 1994, he moved from the linguistics department at the University of Southern California to the School of Education. In a sense, we need two versions of these ideas, one for scientists and one for an audience with less specialized knowledge.

OUTPUT

Virtually no empirical evidence for the usefulness of practice in production exists yet, and certainly no precise documentation of the process of automatization of rules through such practice.

———————

DeKeyser, 1997, p. 198

The most widely accepted version of Skill Acquisition Theory (SAT) was developed by psychologist, John R. Anderson, and is called the Adaptive Control of Thought (ACT) theory (it has been revised multiple times since the first version in 1976). According to the ACT model, declarative knowledge (e.g., facts) is first learned, then procedural knowledge (e.g., skills) is learned, and the procedural knowledge becomes more automatic with practice. SAT is not a theory specific to the study of second language acquisition (SLA). Perhaps the researcher best known for the application of SAT to SLA is psychologist, Robert DeKeyser.

SAT in SLA studies the ability to use a pedagogical grammar, i.e., textbook rules. In other words, it focuses on a non-native type of knowledge, rather than the mental grammar that is the subject of study of linguists and the subject of SLA in general. The theory does not explain some major facts of SLA, e.g., how learners know more than what is in the input (i.e., the logical problem) and why learners follow similar stages of acquisition (i.e., the developmental problem), but again, the object of study of SAT is different.

There is considerable overlap between SAT and mainstream classroom approaches, e.g., the Presentation-Practice-Production (PPP) model (Byrne, 1976) and the drill sequence from Paulston (1970) of mechanical drills (i.e., no meaning required, such as past tense verb conjugation exercises) to meaningful drills (i.e., known-information questions, like "What time did class start?") to so-called communicative drills (e.g., new-information questions with the purpose of practicing language, like "What did you do this weekend?"). However, mainstream approaches are a bad implementation of SAT for multiple reasons, e.g., too much, too fast, not enough meaning-based practice, etc. (e.g., DeKeyser, 2015).

TEXTBOOK GRAMMAR

Despite the best efforts even of highly skilled teachers and textbook writers, focus on forms tends to produce boring lessons, with resulting declines in motivation, attention, and student enrollments. The assertion that many students all over the world have learned languages via a focus on forms ignores the possibility that they have really learned despite it ... as well as the fact that countless others have failed. A focus on forms produces many more false beginners than finishers.

———————

Long, 2000, p. 182

Former classroom learners who have achieved advanced proficiency have most likely been taught textbook rules, been exposed to a lot of language input, had opportunities to produce language, etc. So, how do we sort out causation vs. correlation? Introspection about language learning is problematic. We can reflect on our own learning experiences, but may misattribute progress to the wrong thing.

This quote captures two of the six major problems that Long listed of focus on forms ("forms" with an "s"). This approach presents and models predetermined language pieces one at a time, which the learner is expected to master and put together. This characterizes mainstream instructional practices, e.g., a vocabulary & grammatical syllabus, the Presentation-Practice-Production (PPP) model, and the sequence of mechanical to meaningful to communicative drills.

Long (1991) identified another type of form-focused instruction that he called "focus on form" (FonF). The purpose is to make more input available for acquisition and is not about practicing rules. Form refers to the aural and written shape of language, e.g., *cat* is pronounced[kæt]. FonF briefly draws attention to form (with or without learner awareness) amidst communication. Long intended it to be determined by a learners' current developmental state and reactive to communication problems. Other researchers (e.g., Doughty & Williams, 1998) consider it to include reactive and proactive interventions.

Taking a broad view, there are numerous interventions and techniques under the umbrella of FonF, including but not limited to increasing the frequency of target forms in the input (i.e., input flood), making target forms stand out, for example, by bolding them in a text (i.e., input enhancement), rephrasing a learner's ungrammatical utterance (i.e., recasts), and manipulating input in ways that push learners to link meaning to certain forms (i.e., processing instruction). Only processing instruction has consistently shown positive results.

A lot of research investigates forms that have little to no impact on communication (i.e., low to zero communicative value), which is one reason they are a challenge to acquire. In my view, if the goal is communicative ability (i.e., proficiency), then FonF is like bringing a squirt gun to a pool party. If you want to get soaked, just jump in the pool that is comprehension-based, communicative language teaching.

COMMUNICATION

Current perceptions of the term 'communicative' held by many instructors, textbook authors, and others in the field are most likely a result of two tightly integrated processes. The first is the adaptation of the term 'communicative' to fit traditional beliefs about grammar, vocabulary, language learning, and language teaching. The second is the internalization by practitioners of how they perceive that communicative language teaching is realized in existing textbooks.

VanPatten, 1998, p. 929

To take one example of a misconception, a communicative approach is often equated with group work, but, as one of the founders of communicative language teaching (CLT) makes clear, "CLT does not require small group or pair work" (Savignon, 2017, p. 5).

EDUCATION

According to the qualitative data from this study, the overriding factor [57.3%] hindering instructor decisions to provide target language input for their students involve areas that show lack of teacher preparation and training.

Ceo-DiFrancesco, 2013, p. 7

Week 6

INPUT

That is, the input necessary for language acquisition must contain meaning to which the learner attends for its propositional content.

VanPatten & Cadierno, 1993b, p. 46

OUTPUT

After over a decade of research into Swain's (1985) comprehensible output (CO) hypothesis, there is still a severe lack of data showing that learner output or output modifications have any effect on second-language (L2) learning.

———————

Shehadeh, 2002, p. 597

DUAL SYSTEMS

In the last thirty years, there has been no substantial evidence in SLA to counter the idea that metalinguistic ability is quite different from the main object of study and that a typical use of metagrammatical knowledge, i.e., overt correction of learner output by either teacher of learners themselves, has any tangible effect on syntactic and phonological development.

Sharwood Smith, 2004, p. 275

COMMUNICATION

Communication, then, is a continuous process of expression, interpretation, and negotiation of meaning . . . applies to both written and spoken language . . . is context specific. . . dependent on the roles of the participants, the situation, and the goal of the interaction.

———————

Savignon, 1997, p. 14, 15, 28

Lee and VanPatten (2003) added that communication occurs for two purposes: to build and maintain relationships (i.e., psychosocial) and to learn and exchange new information (i.e., cognitive-informational). VanPatten (2017) added another purpose: to entertain. A lot of the reading we do, television we watch, and games that we play are for the purpose of entertainment. How should a communicative classroom balance the time spent on activities that serve different communicative purposes?

BELIEFS

The historical evidence and modern thought on how change happens concur that the creation of new materials and methods is insufficient. Rather, the second language teaching profession must effect a decisive change in beliefs about how second languages are learned.

Musumeci, 1997, p. 132

Fullan (1992) identified these three components (i.e., procedures, materials, beliefs) as requisites for educational reform. Musumeci's review of the history of language teaching came to the same conclusion. One of her recommendations was for textbooks and methods books to explain their underlying theoretical framework. Learning about language acquisition is necessary, but is sometimes not sufficient to change teachers' beliefs and it is not enough to implement new practices. That is where experience – as a student, observer, and a teacher of a new approach – is necessary so as to create a new "familiar."

Week 7

INPUT

... input is the primary causative variable in second language acquisition, affective variables acting to impede or facilitate the delivery of input to the language acquisition device.

Krashen, 1982, p. 32

In my work in language acquisition, I have concluded that we acquire language in only one way: by understanding messages, or obtaining 'comprehensible input' in a low-anxiety situation.

Krashen, 2004, p. 37

CORRECTION

Direct error correction by the instructor does not promote linguistic accuracy and the absence of error correction in the early stages of acquisition does not impede the development of linguistic accuracy... This finding is perhaps the single most provocative finding for language teachers. Usually, it evokes argument... It is likely that there are some readers who at this moment find themselves in disagreement with the statement before a presentation of the research has even begun.

VanPatten, 1986, p. 212-213

TEXTBOOK GRAMMAR

In conclusion, both the classroom studies and the laboratory research reviewed here provide strong evidence for the effectiveness of explicit learning. The main drawback is that most of the outcome measures used allowed for a certain degree of monitoring, which leaves open the possibility that the explicit learning only yielded explicit knowledge, and not the implicit knowledge necessary for accurate and fluent spontaneous production.

DeKeyser, 1994, p. 88

That is just one of the big qualifiers on instructed SLA research. Unfortunately, it's not too hard to find statements in the literature akin to the first sentence, but that leave out the second sentence.

VOCABULARY

... the topic-based focus of many materials means that low-frequency vocabulary regularly gets explicit attention...

———————

Schmitt & Schmitt, 2012, p. 25

The frequency ranking of a word is an indication of its importance and usefulness. Higher frequency words are those that occur more often and across a wider variety of contexts. Textbooks commonly present words in semantic sets (also known as lexical sets or semantic clusters), i.e., groups of words with related meanings and mostly of the same part of speech (e.g., colors, foods, animals, body, etc.). To get a sense for the frequency of these words, I have selected two words from these sets, one of higher and the other of lower frequency relative to the other members of the set, and listed the frequency ranking (according to Davies' (2006) Spanish frequency dictionary): white (250), orange (8225), meat (787), carrot (7602), horse (780), elephant (4945), hand (150), ear (2407). From the numbers 1-20, only the numbers 1 and 2 are in the most-frequently used 100 words. There are more than 300 words that are more frequent than the numbers 6 through 10, and the numbers 13 through 19 are not in the most frequently used 1,000 Spanish words.

BELIEFS

Articles in pedagogy journals and commercially published textbook materials both reveal what most language teachers already know: recipes for language teaching are two a penny. Some are based on years of classroom experience, precious few on theory or research findings in SLA or education, and many on little more than chutzpah and the pundit's or publisher's desire for a healthier bank balance.

Long, 2009, p. 374

Have you ever wondered whether textbooks got it right? Have you ever questioned the textbook syllabus?

Week 8

INPUT

... comprehensible input in SLA theory is like edible input in a theory of digestion – a given. The problem is to get beyond such platitudes to see how comprehensible input works.

Gregg, 1997, p. 81

Gregg is *the* critic in the field of SLA. Of the critiques of Krashen's model, his are the most cited. He also writes on the topic of what an SLA theory needs to be and that was largely the focus of his critique of Krashen's model. Gregg (e.g., 1996) reminds us of the two central observations that any complete theory of SLA needs to explain: the logical problem (Hornstein & Lightfoot, 1981) and the developmental problem (Felix, 1984). The logical problem asks how it is possible to know more than what learners have been exposed to (also known as the poverty of the stimulus problem). The answer requires a theory of language, i.e., the "what." The developmental problem is about why it is that learners follow universal stages of acquisition, i.e., the "how."

You probably cannot find an introductory SLA book that does not outline Krashen's model, along with mention of the critiques from Gregg and McLaughlin. However, these critics were not arguing for rule-based instruction. Rather, the primary problems had to do with terms that were loosely and/or inconsistently defined, the use of indirect evidence, the lack of explanation for the steps between comprehensible input and acquisition, and the lack of a theory of the nature of the knowledge that winds up in the learner's head.

In a way, Krashen's model was like a description of photosynthesis that says plants need water (comprehensible input) and sunlight (positive affect) to grow (acquire). That's useful knowledge for a gardener (teacher), but scientists want to know more about the interaction between the properties of liquid (input) and the internal properties of plants (nature of language) that lead to growth.

Some teachers know that Krashen was criticized for saying that acquisition is unconscious (McLaughlin, 1978), which some then use to justify a belief that acquisition happens consciously. The actual critique was that the terms needed to be operationalized (made measurable) without recourse to introspection, e.g., subjective experience of communicating by "rule" or "feel." McLaughlin recommended doing away with the conscious/unconscious distinction, at least until we had a theory of mind that would allow us to distinguish them.

CORRECTION

Can a case be made that correction works? Clearly and unambiguously not. In fact, the L2 evidence fits very well with that from the L1 studies; correction is clearly ineffective.

———————

Truscott, 1996, p. 330

This conclusion is in reference to written grammar correction. Regarding oral grammar correction, it is well-known that parents typically only correct children when they make a false statement and attempts to correct their grammar are made in vain (e.g., Brown & Hanlon, 1970). In fact, there are some funny examples that have been documented of this failure of grammar correction (e.g., McNeill, 1966; Pinker, 1994). Correction is negative evidence, i.e., information about what is ungrammatical. Children acquire a first language based entirely on input, i.e., positive evidence. The same ought to be true of a second language, if the two processes are fundamentally similar.

TEXTBOOK GRAMMAR

Thus, in the current domain, over 90% of the dependent variables required the application of L2 rules in highly focused and discrete ways, while only around 10% of the dependent variables required relatively free productive use of the L2. In addition, most primary research has operationalized implicit treatments in relatively restricted ways, whereas explicit treatments often involve combinations of several instructional components.

———————

Norris & Ortega, 2000, p. 483

This comes from the first meta-analysis of instructed SLA research, which was 112 pages long! Only 49 studies met the criteria for inclusion in the analysis (e.g., treatments targeted specific forms and functions and studies of pronunciation and vocabulary were excluded). This meta-analysis is often cited in support of explicit instruction, despite numerous limitations of the studies being analyzed. Explicit instruction was defined as teaching rules, either by explaining rules (i.e., deductive) or instructing learners to figure out the rules on their own (i.e., inductive).

COMMUNICATIVE TESTS

I put the development of new kinds of tests at the top of the list because of the importance of tests in shaping all that we do and think in the classroom... If we teach for communicative competence, we have to test for communicative competence...

Savignon, 1976, p. 5

Savignon's 1972 study is cited as the start of the communicative movement in testing (e.g., Brown, 1996). The tests used in that study were exemplary for the varied contexts of unfamiliar topics used to evaluate proficiency so as to arrive at a more comprehensive assessment. The evaluation criteria involved a mix of objective (e.g., number of correct facts) and subjective measures (e.g., fluency ratings on a 6-point scale).

BELIEFS

Publishing is a competitive business and publishers need to sell their products. Thus, there is a cycle of teachers' perceptions and expectations that shape what publishers will produce. These materials in turn reinforce teachers' perceptions and expectations and the cycle is difficult to break.

VanPatten, 1998, p. 930

Setting aside the decision of textbooks to focus on textbook grammar, as opposed to mental grammar, consider *what* rules and *how many* rules are included.

Take the subjunctive, for example. Collentine (2010) analyzed a corpus of about 20 million words from oral and written samples from native Spanish speakers and found that the subjunctive made up 7.2% of all verb forms. Similarly, in 30-minute interviews, Geeslin and Gudmestad (2010) found that of conjugated verbs, L1 Spanish speakers used the subjunctive 6.7% of the time and advanced L2 Spanish speakers used it 2%

of the time. Now, consider what percentage of those subjunctive uses are necessary for successful communication. Its low frequency and low communicative value, among other reasons, explain why research finds the subjunctive to be late-acquired.

However, what are teacher beliefs about teaching the subjunctive and expectations for student learning? And where do those beliefs and expectations come from? As Collentine (2010) wrote, ". . . contemporary textbooks still give teachers and learners the impression that the subjunctive is so important to communicative goals that its study deserves large proportions of textbook pages and class time" (p. 39). How well would a level 3 or 4 Spanish textbook sell if it no longer tried to teach the subjunctive?

Week 9

INPUT

This study helps to define which approaches to language instruction provide an environment that is rich in potentially comprehensible input. Other things being equal, those classrooms that encourage spoken interaction among participants, so that both teachers and students feel confident to initiate discussion of unclear points, will help to make input comprehensible.

————————

Pica, Young, & Doughty, 1987, p. 754

The impetus of the original interaction hypothesis (Long, 1981) was that interaction makes input more comprehensible. This was the first study to directly test the hypothesis. Comprehension was assessed by giving learners directions as to which object to select and where on a board (depicting an outdoor scene) to put it. The participants who interacted with a native speaker during the task demonstrated greater comprehension than those who received level-appropriate input without interaction. The opportunity for the learners to negotiate meaning (e.g., ask for clarification) got the learners more repetitions of key objects and places.

DEVELOPMENT

SLA theorists can differ not only in their epistemological commitments, but in their view of the domain of SLA theory: what is an SLA theory a theory of? ... No one, however, has presented a coherent argument against the position that second language acquisition involves individual mental states and their changes, so I think that we can accept that position as a working definition of the domain of SLA theory.

———————

Gregg, 2003, p. 835

Gregg's statement was made, in part, in response to those who view SLA as a social, rather than a cognitive phenomenon. Also, note that the study of SLA is not the same as the study of how to best teach languages. However, language teachers benefit from knowing the "what" and the "how" of SLA.

TEXTBOOK GRAMMAR

Taking together biases in approach to and duration of L2 instruction, and the demonstrated biases in measurement, the reported apparent advantage for explicit instruction has more properly been interpreted as an artifact of cumulative research bias. More specifically, all that can be said at present is that, when the outcome of very short-term, explicitly focused instruction is measured on language manipulations tasks, it has proven effective.

———————

Doughty, 2004, p. 198

In sum, the case for explicit instruction has been overstated. In addition, given that only 30% of studies have employed implicit pedagogic techniques, and that outcome measures have been severely biased toward constrained construction, language manipulation, and the assessment of declarative knowledge (90% of measures), any advantages for implicit instruction have likely been understated. In other words, under the present biased research conditions, any observed effects of implicit instruction are remarkable indeed!

———————

Doughty, 2004, p. 199

Interestingly, Doughty was one of Norris and Ortega's professors, her graduate seminar was inspiration for their meta-analysis, and she provided them with feedback on their paper prior to publication. Limitations of studies from Norris and Ortega's (2000) meta-analysis was the main focus of Doughty's chapter critique of instructed SLA research. These limitations are often overlooked and the case for explicit instruction overstated (see examples below). Unqualified interpretations and overstatements have also been made regarding a follow-up meta-analysis (Spada & Tomita, 2010), despite similar limitations that preclude such conclusions.

. . . whether or not (explicit) instruction led to L2 development. . . Extensive research since the 1980s, and Norris and Ortega's et al. (2000) meta-analysis in particular, however, has largely put this debate to rest.

Lee, Jang, & Plonsky, 2015, p. 346

Indeed, empirical research strongly suggests that explicit grammar instruction facilitates L2 development (Norris & Ortega, 2000; Spada & Tomita, 2010).

Toth & Davin, 2016, p. 163

. . . particularly the Norris and Ortega (2000) comprehensive meta-analysis of the last 20 years' empirical work, demonstrated that focused L2 instruction results in large target-oriented gains, that explicit types of instruction are more effective than implicit types, and that the effectiveness of L2 instruction is durable.

N. Ellis, 2002, p. 175

COMMUNICATION

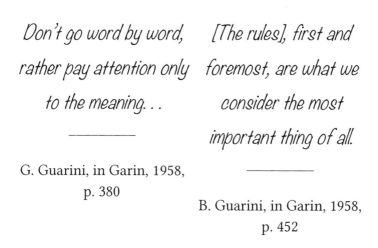

Don't go word by word, rather pay attention only to the meaning...

———

G. Guarini, in Garin, 1958, p. 380

[The rules], first and foremost, are what we consider the most important thing of all.

———

B. Guarini, in Garin, 1958, p. 452

Guarino Guarini (1374-1460) was one of the best-known advocates of the *studia humanitatis* (Latin immersion schooling). He tutored a prince, opened his own school, and was famous for being an effective teacher of Latin and Greek. He did not write any texts on teaching. We know his thoughts through his letters to students. Battista Guarini, his son, wrote his father's thoughts on education in a treatise in 1459. However, the treatise misrepresented his father's ideas, perhaps the first documented example in the history of language teaching of ideas about language learning mistranslated in practice.

PRINCIPLES

The Fundamental Principle applied to pedagogy is as follows: Any instructional technique that helps second language acquisition does so by providing CI [comprehensible input].

––––––––––

Krashen, 1981, p. 59

Week 10

INPUT

For beginners, the classroom can be much better than the outside world, since the outside usually provides the beginner with very little comprehensible input, especially for older acquirers.

———————

Krashen, 1982, p. 30

The quality of the input is also one reason why non-classroom adult learners may not progress as quickly or as far in their acquisition of a second language.

DEVELOPMENT

We have been reminded recently of Von Humboldt's statement that we cannot really teach language, we can only create conditions in which it will develop spontaneously in the mind in its own way. We shall never improve our ability to create such favourable conditions until we learn more about the way a learner learns and what his built-in syllabus is. . . We may be able to allow the learner's innate strategies to dictate our practice and determine our syllabus; we may learn to adapt ourselves to his needs rather than impose upon him our preconceptions of how he ought to learn, what he ought to learn and when he ought to learn it.

Corder, 1967, p. 169

This is a very famous quote from a paper that is often cited as the start to the contemporary field of SLA. From that paper came the distinction between input and what gets taken in, i.e., intake.

TEXTBOOK GRAMMAR

It may very well be that previous research is limited because both the grammar that has been taught and the manner in which it has been taught do little to affect the processes that underlie acquisition.

———————

VanPatten & Cadierno, 1993b, p. 45

This comes from the pilot study of an intervention (not a method) called processing instruction (PI). Processing refers to linking forms to meanings (e.g., the written form *cat* is linked to something like "4-legged, furry pet") and assigning sentence structure (e.g., subject-verb-object). VanPatten's (e.g., 1996, 2004, 2015b) model of second language input processing identifies strategies that guide interpretation, e.g., the First-Noun Principle (FNP) is the tendency to process the first noun or pronoun as the subject (which will be a problem in languages that permit flexible word order). Input frequency won't matter if forms are being inaccurately processed or not processed at all. Thus, PI focuses on the first step (i.e., converting input to intake) in constructing a mental grammar. The bulk of the classic PI treatment consists of structured input activities that promote accurate input processing. For example, an item from an activity aimed at correcting the FNP may have the participant match a sentence to one of two pictures in which the only difference is who is doing what to whom. The only feedback provided would be whether the selection was right or wrong.

COMMUNICATION

. . . rule-governed practice may not have been nearly as widely prescribed as the historical summaries suggest. Instead, the rote teaching of forms and rules has consistently coexisted with a concomitant insistence on language as communication and the privileged status of attention to meaning in the acquisition process. The tension between treating the second language as the object of instruction versus a system of communication has persisted throughout the history of language teaching, with the former often a by-product of external, pragmatic forces rather than an instantiation of theoretical stance.

Musumeci, 2009, p. 44

PRINCIPLES

I agree with him that most language learning is unconscious, that comprehensible input is vital for learning and that a teacher's most important job is to provide that input, that affective barriers can prevent successful acquisition of a second language and that a teacher has the duty to try to lower those barriers whenever possible. But then, does anybody disagree?

Gregg, 1984, p. 94

The #1 critic of Krashen's model agreed with the pedagogical implications. Notice the intentional use of "barrier" as opposed to "filter." Rather than motivation, anxiety, etc. selectively allowing some comprehended input in and filtering out other input, the learner who is unmotivated, anxious, etc. will seek out fewer opportunities to be exposed to input and may at times block input from being processed.

Week 11

INPUT

The most marked difference occurred at the highest level of usage with only 10.5% of the instructors reporting actual utilization of the target language 90-100% of the time compared to 40.9% stating this rate as their goal. Similar numbers of respondents reported actual target language use for nearly all rate ranges.

Ceo-DiFrancesco, 2013, p. 4

The rate ranges started at 20-30% reported target language use and increased by 10% intervals. This says nothing about whether the teacher's input is communicative and comprehensible. In a study of English second language (ESL) teachers, Long and Sato (1983) found that teachers ask a lot more display questions (about known info, e.g., "What color is your shirt?") than referential questions (about new information, e.g., "What do you like to wear?"). The reverse was the case of conversations that occurred with learners outside of the classroom. The purpose of display questions is not communicative. Rather, it is to teach and test language. The researchers concluded, "communicative use of the target language makes up only a minor part of typical classroom activities" (p. 280).

DEVELOPMENT

Furthermore, this common sequence indicates that the learning order of these structures is controlled by the child's processing strategies, in the sense that he must be cognitively 'ready' in order to acquire any one of them.

———————

Dulay & Burt, 1973, p. 256

Evidence of first language acquisition orders had been collected prior to this study, but published in the same year (Brown, 1973; de Villiers & de Villiers, 1973). Dulay and Burt (1973) were the first to document an acquisition order in SLA, as well as finding a similar order among learners of different first languages (Dulay & Burt, 1974b).

The forms investigated are called morphemes, which refer to the smallest units of grammatical meaning. Specifically, they examined grammatical morphemes (e.g., articles, verb endings, etc.). Although both the present progressive (*-ing*) and the third person singular present (*-s*) are taught early in level 1 of a textbook grammar and both occur frequently in the input, can you guess which is early and which is late-acquired?

59

Language use was assessed (as it commonly is in developmental pattern research) with a spontaneous and unrehearsed oral task called the Bilingual Syntax Measure. It consists of answering questions about pictures.

Research on the development of output looks at the order in time by which structures are first used (i.e., emergence), the relative accuracy of structures, and/or the time at which a structure passes a certain threshold of accuracy.

DUAL SYSTEMS

The hypothesis to be defended is that negative data [feedback that a learner's utterance is incorrect] and explicit data result in a type of knowledge that is not to be equated with linguistic competence. The claim is not that negative and explicit data cannot give rise to knowledge; rather, the specific claim is that only positive data [input] can effect the construction of an interlanguage grammar that is comparable to the knowledge system that characterizes the result of first language acquisition.

Schwartz, 1993, p. 147

Schwartz distinguished "learned linguistic knowledge" from "linguistic competence." Schwartz is also a leading proponent of full access in SLA to Universal Grammar, i.e., innate principles that also guide first language acquisition.

COMMUNICATION

In our concern for 'respectability' and, subsequently, for norms and standardization of achievement criteria, we have remained prisoners of academia and failed to offer our students the kinds of language learning experiences they need most.

———————

Savignon, 1976, p. 13-14

PRINCIPLES

Thus, a method is theoretically related to an approach, is organizationally determined by a design, and is practically realized in procedure.

Richards & Rodgers, 2014, p. 22

Before we can talk about different methods, we need to define "method." Richards and Rodgers modified and added to Anthony's (1963) model for conceptualizing a method. In the Richard and Rodger's framework, a method encompasses three levels. Approach refers to principles derived of research and theory, design is how the program is organized, and procedure is what happens every day in the classroom. In other words, contrary to how many people use the word, method refers to much more than classroom procedures.

Week 12

INPUT

Learners who receive instruction that attempts to alter input processing receive a double bonus: better processing of input and knowledge that is apparently also available for production.

VanPatten & Cadierno, 1993a, p. 240

This sums up the big finding of the intervention called processing instruction (PI). The improvement in output happens although the participants never produce the target form. On the contrary, participants receiving so-called "traditional instruction" (rules presentation + production practice) only make improvements in production. This study launched a line of research, which to date has yielded 80+ studies (for a review, see, e.g., Wong & VanPatten, 2003). It may very well be that no other instructional intervention has been so well-researched, nor provided more consistently positive results.

DEVELOPMENT

Of the hundreds of studies of interlanguage (IL) development now completed, not one shows either tutored [classroom] or naturalistic [non-classroom] learners developing proficiency one linguistic item at a time. On the contrary, all reveal complex, gradual and inter-related developmental paths for grammatical subsystems... Moreover, development is not unidirectional; omission/suppliance of forms fluctuates, as does accuracy of suppliance.

Long, 1991, p. 44

Almost thirty years ago, it was already abundantly clear that linguistic items are not learned and mastered one at a time. Rather, multiple aspects of language are gradually being learned at the same time and learners don't abruptly move to the next stage and leave the previous stage entirely behind. Furthermore, learners progress at different rates and progress occurs between periods of apparent stabilization, i.e., plateaus (Harley & Swain, 1984).

65

DUAL SYSTEMS

... the 'no-interface' idea of two distinct kinds of language knowledge with one type, consciously learned knowledge about language, exerting no direct influence on the growth of the other type, intuitive knowledge, has proved quite robust over the years.

———————

Sharwood Smith & Truscott, 2014a, p. 258

COMMUNICATION

Comprehension is inherently communicative, and comprehension-oriented classroom techniques are always potentially communicative in nature. . . On the other hand, much oral practice - at least as commonly used in the classroom - is manipulative rather than communicative.

———————

Gary & Gary, 1981, p. 336-337

BELIEFS

Clearly, method is important only to the extent that teachers understand the principles of language learning that underscore it.

———————

Musumeci, 1997, p. 128

What happens when teachers learn new activities, but don't change their beliefs about how languages are acquired? Are teacher practices and materials that are labeled "communicative" compatible with principles of a communicative approach? For example, one of Savignon's principles is that "Formal accuracy in the beginning stages should be neither required nor expected" (1997, p. 29). Actually, that is a good principle for language use at any level of proficiency, not just the "beginning stages." Improvements in accuracy are gradual, non-linear, and, in some areas, performance may not ever be the same as native speakers.

Week 13

MENTAL GRAMMAR

The second-language learner who actually achieves native-like competence cannot possibly have been taught this competence, since linguists are daily – in almost every generative study – discovering new and fundamental facts about particular languages. Successful learners, in order to achieve this native-speaker competence, must have acquired these facts (and most probably important principles of language organization) without having explicitly been taught them.

Selinker, 1972, p. 212-213

This very famous paper contributed to the start of the contemporary field of SLA. The title of the paper, "Interlanguage" is a term Selinker coined to refer to the developing language system that is something in between the first and second language systems.

DEVELOPMENT

Learners follow universal stages of development. However, this does not mean that for a given stage of acquisition all learners use identical grammatical systems. Instead, there is a degree of variability in the use of interlanguage systems.

Pienemann, 2011, p. 22

In other words, there are options available for expressing oneself within a given stage of development and learners will make different choices. See Pienemann's work on Processability Theory (e.g., 1998, 2005) to learn of the six stages that describe the development of spontaneous output at the phrasal level. Guess what stage corresponds to subject-verb agreement. . . stage 5. The use of the subjunctive in subordinate clauses belongs to the sixth and final stage. And you can't skip stages.

TEXTBOOK GRAMMAR

Skill Acquisition Theory is most easily
applicable to what happens in
(a) high-aptitude adult learners engaged in
(b) the learning of simple structures at
(c) fairly early stages of learning in
(d) instructional contexts.

———————

DeKeyser, 2015, p. 101

What about the average teenager in a required second language class?

ENJOYMENT

Even if it were shown that conscious learning was as good as acquisition, or even twice as efficient, I would still prefer comprehensible input. . .

———————

Krashen, 1989, p. 454

Motivating obligatory second language learners is a major concern of second language teachers. Krashen's argument is that communicative classrooms providing a lot of comprehensible input are more enjoyable than rule-based classrooms. And enjoyment may be directly related to whether people are motivated to continue their second language education, as well as whether they support it. That is the greater goal of all education, right? To produce life-long learners and supporters. This becomes especially important when exposure to the second language is limited to the classroom, because then there is not enough time for students to reach advanced proficiency.

Early second language (L2) motivation research (e.g., Gardner & Lambert, 1972) focused on integrative motivation (the desire to integrate into the L2 community) and instrumental motivation (learning the language for practical reasons). A classic early semester activity focuses on instrumental motivation by giving students reasons to learn the L2. And when that doesn't work, some teachers resort to extrinsic motivators (rewards and punishments), like grades.

L2 motivation expert, Zoltán Dörnyei, proposed a process-oriented model of motivation that included 3 phases: 1) what you choose to do, 2) engagement during the activity, and 3) how you evaluate the experience (e.g., Dörnyei and Ottó, 1998). In this conceptualization, integrative and instrumental motivation primarily belong to the first phase. However, the keys to learner motivation may lie in the other 2 phases.

Choosing activities and content that are highly engaging increases participation and effort during the activity (i.e., task-specific motivation) and when learners experience success and attribute that to their own abilities, then that boosts self-confidence. This is to say what many of us know intuitively: We like to do what we enjoy and what we are good at. The ultimate result is intrinsic motivation, i.e., participating in the activity is its own reward. Another effect is that more learners will want to be in a second language classroom, which will be reflected by student retention in the program.

PRINCIPLES

Thus it is NOT a question of "from linguistic competence to communicative competence" but rather of from communicative competence to linguistic competence, if that is where you want to go. It is not a question of patching up existing programs with "communication practice drills," "pseudo-communication," but of redefining our goals and rethinking our methods.

————————

Savignon, 1976, p. 3

Hymes (1972), a sociolinguist, introduced the term communicative competence. Canale and Swain (1980), refined by Canale (1983), identified 4 different competencies that make up communicative competence: grammatical (sounds, word order, and meaning) sociolinguistic (what is socially appropriate in a given context), discourse (coherent combination of sentences), and strategic (verbal and non-verbal handling of communication breakdowns due to lack of knowledge, i.e., coping strategies). Nowadays, proficiency has largely replaced the term communicative competence.

Week 14

MENTAL GRAMMAR

We can think of the initial state of the faculty of language as a fixed network connected to a switch box; the network is constituted of the principles of language, while the switches are the options to be determined by experience... Each possible human language is identified as a particular setting of the switches... Notice that small changes in switch settings can lead to great apparent variety in output, as the effects proliferate through the system.

Chomsky, 2000, p.8

Noam Chomsky is the father of modern linguistics and what is called generative grammar. Generative, because sentences are *generated* by a set of mental "rules." The "rules" bear no resemblance to textbook rules and are better thought of as abstract properties.

Chomsky put forward the first iteration of generative grammar in 1957 and began his case for Universal Grammar (UG) in 1959. UG refers to the abstract, language-specific properties that we are born with and as such, they do not have to be learned. UG limits the options of possible languages, which is to be argued what makes the task of language learning easier and possible. Despite differences in environment and intelligence and without formal instruction, all children acquire language before they can do basic addition and before they can tie their shoes. Hence why this perspective views language as truly special and unlike the learning of other things.

The switch box metaphor helps us conceptualize UG. For example, sentences consist of hierarchically-ordered phrases and every type of phrase - both content-word phrases (e.g., verb phrases) and grammatical-word phrases (e.g., tense phrases) - has the same basic structure in every language. There is a key word (e.g., "under") and two types of optional modifiers (e.g., "*right* under *there*"). This principle of phrase structure does not have to be learned. Languages can differ as to the position of the key word. In Japanese, it would be "right there under," which means this is a postpositional phrase.

Input flips the switches, which were called "parameters" under the Principles and Parameters framework (Chomsky, 1981) and now seen as (parametrized) "features" that have either a strong or a weak value under the Minimalist Program (Chomsky, 1995). The effect of input on UG grows what generative linguists call "language." In principle, a single exposure is enough to trigger a UG setting. In reality, acquisition is gradual. See Sharwood Smith and Truscott (2005) for one way of reconciling a linguistic perspective with the gradual nature of acquisition.

Linguistic perspectives in SLA traditionally focused on access or not to UG (a matter largely settled 2 decades ago in the affirmative, at least regarding access to some properties of UG). The field then shifted to explaining L1-L2 differences that were not caused by lack of UG access.

OUTPUT

Immersion students become quite fluent in the target language and are generally able to communicate what they need and want to say in the academic context of their classroom... we tape-recorded a day in the life of ten grade 6 immersion classes, and we discovered that there was surprisingly little French spoken by the students that was of any significant length... We also found that feedback from the teachers on errors the students made, although not infrequent, seemed haphazard and random...

Swain & Lapkin, 1995, p. 372

So, how did fluency and communicative ability develop?

TEXTBOOK GRAMMAR

Latin grammar was taught us with all the exceptions and irregularities; Greek grammar with all its dialects, and we, poor wretches, were so confused that we scarcely understood what it was all about.

Comenius, 1657, p. 122

Even when learners do learn the rules, as learners and teachers everywhere can probably attest and research has confirmed, that does not mean learners can use the rules (e.g., Terrell, Baycroft, & Perrone, 1987) and whatever knowledge is gained in the short-term is often forgotten (e.g., Harley, 1989; White, 1991). Hence the importance of research that includes communicative tests a few months after the treatment.

COMMUNICATION

An authentic text is a stretch of real language, produced by a real speaker or writer for a real audience and designed to convey a real message of some sort.

———

Morrow, 1977, p. 13

The term "authentic" is emotionally loaded (Cook, 1997), often poorly defined, and undertheorized. Gilmore (2007) identified at least 8 different meanings of the word. If authentic gets defined as for-native-speakers-by-native-speakers, then all interaction between teachers and language learners would be inauthentic. Texts that have been written for native speakers and not language learners are better labeled "ungraded" or "unleveled" texts. We can do away with the term "authentic" and just talk about what is real. But since people often say "real world" when they mean "outside of the classroom," (the classroom *is* part of the real world) maybe it's best we just talk about what is level-appropriate and communicative.

PRINCIPLES

The best methods are therefore those that supply comprehensible input in low anxiety situations, containing messages that students really want to hear. These methods do not force early production in the second language, but allow students to produce when they are 'ready,' recognizing that improvement comes from supplying communicative and comprehensible input, and not from forcing and correcting production.

———

Krashen, 1982, p. 7

Week 15

MENTAL GRAMMAR

Perhaps the most important implication of generative grammar for second language pedagogy was that the grammatical descriptions used for constructing syllabuses or practice materials were hopelessly inadequate as descriptions of the internal system which learners had to develop in order to achieve grammatical accuracy in their language use. It was therefore unlikely that any planned progression in a grammatical syllabus could actually reflect or regulate the development of the internal grammatical system being aimed at.

Prabhu, 1987, p. 17

OUTPUT

The best way, and perhaps the only way, to teach speaking, according to this view, is simply to provide comprehensible input.

———————

Krashen, 1982, p. 22

Input is needed to construct the mental grammar that underlies the "four skills" (listening, speaking, reading, writing).

TEXTBOOK GRAMMAR

The conundrum for the textbook writer – and the paradox of teaching grammar at all – is that if the grammar is simple enough to teach, it's inaccurate; yet if it is complex enough to be accurate, it's impractical to teach.

———————

Murphy & Hastings, 2006, p. 11

There are numerous exceptions to textbook rules, because they are not anything like the "rules," or rather, the abstract properties of a mental grammar. Textbook rules are generalizations about the result of an application of abstract "rules." In other words, a textbook grammar doesn't describe the rules that actually underlie native language use (i.e., use of a mental grammar).

Nor is mental grammar anything like a prescriptive grammar, which are the rules taught in school about how we should talk/write, e.g., don't end a sentence with a preposition. This example may be considered "bad grammar" by some arbitrary standard, established by the elite and often based on Latin (e.g., preposition stranding is ungrammatical in Latin), but it is not ungrammatical in English. If it were ungrammatical, then people wouldn't say it. In other words, a mental grammar describes what people actually say, not what someone thinks they should say.

83

COMMUNICATION

Above all, remember that for it to be real, communication must be a personalized, spontaneous event. It cannot be programmed - but you can make it happen.

―――――――――

Savignon, 1976, p. 20

The moment-to-moment adjustments that teachers make to be comprehensible and communicate about what is meaningful to students requires a certain amount of personalization and spontaneity. Savignon (1997) would make two of her six principles of a communicative approach about personalized learning (also known as "differentiation" in general education): "L2 learning, like L1 learning, begins with the needs and interests of the learner" and "An analysis of learner needs and interests provides the most effective basis for materials development" (p. 29).

PRINCIPLES

Krashen is, of course, right that we should be cautious about how we manipulate the input, since we often do not know what input is relevant to a particular learner. It is true that we have, as yet, very little idea of how the input interacts with the learner's internalized system, and it might be useful to take some of Krashen's proposals not so much as a theory but as guidelines on how to behave in the absence of a theory, i.e. behave as if the input will contain structures relevant to i+1 [the learner's next level of competence].

———

White, 1987, p. 108

White is a leading proponent of full access in SLA to Universal Grammar, and, as such, supports the causative role of input in SLA. In this critique paper, White takes issue with some aspects of the input hypothesis and tries to "tighten up Krashen's formulation" (p. 95). However, she accepts Krashen's formulation as a guiding pedagogical principle.

White agrees that input should not be grammatically sequenced, which was part three (of four) of the input hypothesis (Krashen, 1982). This corollary was later named by Krashen and Terrell (1983) the "net hypothesis," because when learners get a lot of input, it "casts a net" around what is relevant to a learner's current state.

There are multiple reasons for why this a good practical guideline for classroom practice. For instance, learners acquire at different rates and, therefore, are at different stages, so input relevant to one learner may not be relevant to the next. It is impractical (if not impossible) to know the current state of every student's interlanguage. Trying to grammatically sequence the input restrains (if not prevents) communication. Etc.

Week 16

MENTAL GRAMMAR

It must be said, however, that most studies conducted within a generative framework would argue very strongly that L2 grammars are UG-constrained...

———————

Mitchell, Myles, & Marsden, 2013, p. 90

...evidence in support of adult accessibility to (at least some properties of) UG (e.g., evidence of true PoS in L2 acquisition) had reached a critical mass (see White, 2003) by the early 2000s.

———————

Rothman & Slabakova, 2018, p. 423

Poverty of the stimulus (PoS) cases in SLA are those showing learners knowing more than what is in the input that also couldn't come from first language knowledge, general learning ability, nor instruction. This includes knowing when sentences are ungrammatical, even though we have never heard the sentences before and no one has ever told us that the sentences are ungrammatical. This leaves only innate knowledge (i.e., Universal Grammar). PoS cases in first and second language acquisition are evidence that the two processes are fundamentally similar.

Here is one brief and simplified example. Imagine I am talking about my family and what you need to know is that everyone in my family is short. If I said in English "Nobody thinks that he is tall," then it can mean that not one person in my family thinks of himself or herself as being tall. You get the same interpretation if you say the sentence in Spanish but do not pronounce the pronoun for "he," which is allowed in Spanish ("Nadie cree que es alto"). But, if I pronounce the pronoun in Spanish, then the interpretation changes and "he" refers to someone else other than a member in my family.

English speakers learning Spanish at beginning, intermediate, and advanced levels know this and the higher the level, the more native-like they are (Pérez-Leroux & Glass, 1999). But this subtle difference is something they could not have learned from their first language, it is not something they were ever taught, and they were never exposed to the sentence with the incorrect interpretation and were told it was wrong. This restriction on pronoun interpretation exists in all languages that allow pronouns not to be pronounced, such as Spanish and Chinese. Everyone is born with this restriction (i.e., the Overt Pronoun Constraint), but it only becomes active in second language acquisition when the learner processes input from a language that does not pronounce pronouns.

CORRECTION

Corrections do not increase writing accuracy, writing fluency, or general language proficiency, and they may have a negative effect on student attitudes, especially when students must make corrections by themselves.

Semke, 1984, p. 195

This sums up the findings of a well-known error correction study. In addition, students from the correction groups reported avoidance behavior (not using language perceived to be difficult). There were also several instances of cheating in the correction groups, and, when combined with correction, the positive effects of content-based comments were nixed.

TEXTBOOK GRAMMAR

Cazden (1972) suggests that the first paradox in language acquisition is that while the attention of neither parent nor child is focused on language structure, that is what all children learn well. Our personal experience as ESL teachers in the primary grades suggests a 'first paradox' in second language syntax instruction: while the attention of both teacher and child is focused on language structure, much of what is taught in class is not learned and much of what is learned was not taught in class.

Dulay & Burt, 1974a, p. 135

VOCABULARY

... for whatever N number of vocabulary words a textbook includes, only 10-50% of those are among the N most frequent lemma in the language. For example, ... if a textbook presents 2000 vocabulary words, only 10-50% of those words are among the most frequently used 2000 lemma in the language.

Davies & Face, 2006, p. 142

In this study, the words from the end-of-chapter vocabulary lists in six popular, university-level, years one and two textbooks, were compared to Davies' (2006) frequency dictionary. Also, consider the total number of words expected to be learned. All but one of these textbooks had well over 1,000 different lemmas. A lemma includes the base word (e.g., enjoy), inflections of the same part of speech (e.g., enjoys, enjoyed, enjoying), but not derivations (e.g., enjoyment). Native speakers immersed in the native language only acquire about 1,000 word families per year. A word family includes the base word, inflected forms, *and* derivations. Nation, a leading vocabulary researcher, said that written recognition of 1,000 word families, 500 to be conservative, be a goal for motivated adults in a class meeting three-to-four hours/week with two hours of homework/week (personal communication, September 28, 2014).

91

PRINCIPLES

Indeed, it was a pleasant surprise for the project group [the teachers] to realize how far task-based interaction ensured adequate simplification and comprehension without any prior linguistic planning.

Prabhu, 1987, p. 27

Before much (if any) theorizing about tasks had occurred among SLA researchers, a teacher educator, N.S. Prabhu, had already implemented a comprehension-oriented version of task-based teaching of English over a 5-year (1979-1984) period in Southern India. The book he published in 1987 documents the principles and evolution of the procedures used in the project. The project focused on developing a mental grammar and accuracy of language use, Prabhu wrote, "is thought to arise from the operation of some internal system of abstract rules or principles, and it is the development of that system that task-based activity is intended to promote" (p. 70). There was no grammatical syllabus and no group work. Most of class time was spent on whole-class, teacher-guided tasks, followed by students working independently on similar tasks.

Week 17

COMPREHENSION

In practical terms, listening comprehension is of paramount significance. When speaking a language, a learner can manipulate a relatively narrow range of vocabulary at his or her own pace to express an idea, but when listening to the reply he or she no longer controls the choice of vocabulary. . . In order to handle a simple conversation, an individual must have a much broader competency in listening comprehension than in speaking. . .

———

Nord, 1981, p. 69

This comes from a chapter in a book titled *The Comprehension Approach to Foreign Language Instruction.*

Comprehension is sometimes mischaracterized as a "passive skill," but effort often has to be exerted to understand what something means. The often intentional and active nature of the process is perhaps more apparent when referred to as "interpretation."

DEVELOPMENT

Perhaps the most important general conclusion we can draw from first language acquisition research is that the child's errors are not indicators of faulty learning nor of a need for instructional intervention. Rather, making errors is a necessary condition in the learning process.

———

Dulay & Burt, 1974a, p. 135

Dulay and Burt found that the source of the majority of "errors" made by second language acquirers was not the first language. They were developmental forms and similar to structures used by first language learners. "Error" implies the learner could have done better, but what if that is the best he/she can do given the current state of his/her developing language system? Aware of the negative connotations of the term and acknowledging the inevitability, even possible necessity of target language deviations, Dulay and Burt had introduced the new term "goofs" the year prior (appearing in the 1974c publication). The term never caught on. Today, we can avoid "errors" and talk of "developing forms" or "interlanguage forms."

TEXTBOOK GRAMMAR

In particular, the evidence suggests that implicit, immersion-like training leads to more native-like neural processing than explicit, classroom-like training – at retention as well as at end of training.

————————

Morgan-Short, Finger, Grey, & Ullman, 2012, p. 13

Both groups in this study, with and without the rule-based instruction, obtained high average comprehension scores on the word order structures being tested, but brain responses between the two groups were qualitatively different. It took about 10 minutes of teaching rules to obstruct native-like brain activity (which showed up on immediate and 5-month delayed tests), despite the 3.5 hours that everyone spent on meaning-based comprehension and production practice.

RELATIONSHIPS

Responding to the students' writing as in treatment I (with reinforcing responses and questions in the target language, so that students know that they are being understood) results in a student-teacher communication which could play a vital role in building a positive relationship. Probably more than anything else, more than any method, technique, or material used, it is this positive relationship which forms the basis for effective teaching.

———

Semke, 1984, p. 202

This comment refers to the group that received feedback that was content-based (with no correction) and which achieved higher fluency, higher proficiency, and more positive attitudes.

PRINCIPLES

Children can learn new structures from relatively uncontrolled materials, provided there is the support of cues from pictures, absorbing context, and teacher guidance.

———————

Elley & Mangubhai, 1983, p. 66

This is the landmark "book flood" study. Every 4-5 weeks, about 50 more books (in the second language) were given to classrooms (that had very few books) of 4th-6th graders from 6 Fijian and 6 Indian schools, for a total of 250 different books over 8 months and 100 additional books in the 2nd year. During English class (immersion schooling started in the third grade), the students in the shared book group (read-aloud of picture books and follow-up activities) and silent reading groups outperformed the audiolingual group (pattern practice and dialogue memorization) on a range of different tests (including a grammar test of structures taught in the audiolingual program) after the first and second years of the program. The book flood groups also did better on subject matter tests given in their first language.

Week 18

COMPREHENSION

Text comprehension is a complex process, requiring the involvement of many different components, relying upon many different kinds of information, and yielding complex mental representations.

———————

W. Kintsch & Rawson, 2005, p. 225

What is comprehension? Walter Kintsch proposed the construction-integration model of reading comprehension (Kintsch, 1998; Kintsch & van Dijk, 1978), which includes three levels of (interacting) mental representations. The linguistic level includes the "lower-level" processes entailed in constructing propositions (minimal units of meaning). The "higher-level" processes are often divided into two main levels: the textbase level refers to the network of interrelated propositions that form a literal representation of the text and organized around global topics (i.e., the "gist") and the situation model is the integration of the textbase with background knowledge and the goals of the reader, which form the reader's interpretation of the situation.

DEVELOPMENT

... don't expect from a baby's lips the learning appropriate to a mature adult.

———————

G. Guarini, in Garin, 1958, p. 420

... If students don't possess to perfection the elementary notions, the further one progresses the more apparent weaknesses become. Therefore, in the first place, children must learn to decline nouns and to conjugate verbs.

———————

B. Guarini, in Garin, 1958, p. 440

Guarino Guarini's ideas of "accuracy in the end" were misrepresented in his son's treatise as "accuracy first."

DUAL SYSTEMS

...[Sociocultural-based] teaching as well as the knowledge that learners acquire is explicit in nature. To be sure, this implies that learners who have developed an L2 through schooling are psychologically functioning with the language in qualitatively different ways from how they function in their L1, which they acquired primarily in everyday contexts and perhaps even how they acquire L2s in immersion settings.

———

Lantolf, Thorne, & Poehner, 2015, p. 221

[Sociocultural theory in SLA] is very much concerned with concrete classroom activity and its impact on learning. It argues for the pedagogical relevance of explicit and rigorous linguistic explanation, especially that derived from cognitive linguistics, and is devoted to discovering how to make learning happen through direct instruction. It is different from other theories of SLA in that it does not assume that acquisition is a universal process.

———

Lantolf, 2011, p. 43

According to sociocultural theory (SCT), language is a cultural tool that mediates between thought and the social-material world. Development is said to first proceed by regulating our thoughts with objects, then relying on other people, and finally, by thinking on our own. SCT was developed by Russian psychologist, L. S. Vygotsky, in the early 1900s. The first SCT study in SLA was Frawley & Lantolf (1985). James P. Lantolf is the researcher best known for the application of SCT to SLA.

I can repeat what I said about Skill Acquisition Theory, because the same is true of SCT. SCT studies the ability to use textbook rules or, as Lantolf (2011) said, "development of communicatively functional declarative knowledge" (p. 37). The theory does not explain some major facts of SLA, e.g., how learners know more than what is in the input (i.e., the logical problem) and why learners follow universal stages of acquisition (i.e., the developmental problem), but again, the object of study of SCT is different, i.e., the development of a non-native type of knowledge.

Socioculturalists promote the use of concept-based instruction to teach textbook grammar, in particular, a procedure called "Systemic Theoretical Instruction." There are 4 main steps: 1) Verbally explain the rule and compare it to the first language, 2) Represent the rule with diagrams and/or other materials, 3) Practice with exercises & activities, 4) Have learners verbalize their understanding of the rule.

RELATIONSHIPS

The rapport they [students] feel with the teacher as well as with classmates may be crucial in determining the success or failure of the venture [i.e., communicative language teaching].

Savignon, 1997, p. 81

Savignon (1997) said of her 1972 study that greater group rapport was established in the group spending time on communicative activities by allowing occasional use of the L1. Quickly glossing words that are new or forgotten may also help make input more comprehensible. The vast majority of class time should still be spent in the second language, but judicious use of the L1 can make acquisition more efficient and enjoyable.

L1 use is stigmatized and sometimes prohibited in language teaching. This is likely due, in part, to practices in which students spend large amounts of class time translating texts. Another reason is likely the misunderstanding that a similar internal process in L1 and L2 acquisition means that the external conditions should be the same (expressed by software programs as teaching language the "natural way"). However, as bilingual researchers find, the L1 is activated during L2 use. The Revised Hierarchical Model (Kroll & Stewart, 1994) posits that lower proficiency L2 learners access meaning through their L1. In other words, translation happens whether we like it or not.

BELIEFS

What we find in language teaching materials (at all levels, by the way) is simple historical inertia from decades and decades of 'that's how it's done.' Nowhere are language teaching materials genuinely informed by what we know about language and language acquisition, for example, in spite of what publishers may tout in a preface or back cover. Nor are the materials informed by what we know about the development of proficiency.

———————

VanPatten, 2015c, p. 10

Week 19

READING

On the whole, however, it is difficult to escape the conclusion that the critical factors which brought about the substantial improvements were related to greater and repeated exposure to print in high-interest contexts, in conditions where pupils were striving for meaning, and receiving sufficient support to achieve it regularly... Time spent on reading in school has been regarded largely as entertaining, as relaxing. However, it must also be seen now as educationally beneficial.

———

Elley & Mangubhai, 1983, p. 66

DEVELOPMENT

Despite the differences in adult learners in amount of instruction, exposure to English, and mother tongue, there is a high degree of agreement as to the relative difficulty of the set of grammatical morphemes examined here.

———

Bailey, Madden, & Krashen, 1974, p. 240

... relative accuracy in adults is quite similar to the relative accuracies shown by children learning English as a second language...

———

Bailey, Madden, & Krashen, 1974, p. 241-242

This was the first study (followed by many more) to show that the order in which accuracy of grammatical morphemes develops among adult second language learners is very similar to the order found in children acquiring a second language. In addition, this study compared 33 Spanish speakers with 40 speakers from 11 different first languages, as well as comparing learners in all-day classes versus those receiving instruction only 4 hours per week. This is Krashen's most-cited study according to Google Scholar.

Recall that language use in this type of research is assessed with spontaneous and unrehearsed oral tasks. In this case, the task was the Bilingual Syntax Measure, which consists of answering questions about pictures.

Also note that the grammatical forms investigated were surely taught in the ESL classes, some since the first weeks. Yet, the average student from this study would have a failing grade on third person singular verbs (as well as some other forms) and the average student did not reach 90% accuracy on any of the 8 tested forms.

DUAL SYSTEMS

While children acquire the language they are exposed to through a system of cognitive structures whose innate principles are specifically geared to the acquisition of language, in the adult this language-specific cognitive system competes with another largely autonomous cognitive system which operates in general problem-solving tasks and is fundamentally inadequate for the purpose of language acquisition.

———

Felix, 1985, p. 50

Felix (1985) called this the "Competition Model." The idea is that there are two knowledge systems that compete to process input, one language-specific (i.e., Universal Grammar) and one general learning system. Felix proposed that the general learning system cannot be suppressed, which could be one of the reasons why second language learners may not reach a native-like final stage of knowledge.

COMMUNICATION

Camp followers and military attendants, engaged in the kitchen and in other menial occupations, learn a tongue that differs from their own, sometimes two or three, quicker than the children in schools learn Latin only... The former gabble their languages after a few months, while the latter, after fifteen or twenty years can only put a few sentences into Latin with the aid of grammars and of dictionaries, and cannot do even this without mistakes and hesitation. Such a disgraceful waste of time and of labour must assuredly arise from a faulty method.

———————

Comenius, 1657, p. 79

BELIEFS

Finally, the most prevalent problem in narrative reviews arises when reviewers base their conclusions on the conclusions drawn by primary researchers, which, as Long (1983) among others has demonstrated, may have little to do with what the research data actually showed.

———

Norris & Ortega, 2000, p. 424

This is a cautionary statement for reading research. You can't just accept the researcher's interpretation expressed in the abstract and conclusion section without having critically analyzed the methodological design and results. The irony is that this statement comes from Norris and Ortega (2000), which you will recall was a meta-analysis that often gets cited as support for rule-based instruction when the research data actually revealed numerous limitations that preclude such a conclusion.

Besides unqualified conclusions and overstatements, there is sometimes a disconnect between findings and teaching recommendations. This can even come from generative linguists who detail the complexity of a structure, review and add to the evidence that L1 and L2 acquisition are fundamentally similar processes, but then propose that textbooks include more and better grammatical explanations (Gil, Marsden, & Whong, 2019; Marsden & Slabakova, 2019).

Week 20

READING

… I consider that the single most important change a teacher could make to a language course is to have a substantial extensive reading program.

Nation, 2016, p. 305

"Extensive reading (ER) has been implemented under a wide variety of names, such as *(uninterrupted) sustained silent reading, free voluntary reading, pleasure reading, book flood, independent reading,* and *Drop Everything And Read (DEAR)*; its various names emphasize different aspects of the same/similar kind of reading." (Yamashita, 2015, p. 168). A meta-analysis of 49 studies that conformed to 5 of the 10 principles of extensive reading outlined in Day & Bamford (1998, revised in 2002) found small to medium effect sizes on English as a second language reading proficiency (Jeon & Day, 2016). ER as part of a language course, as opposed to part of a reading course, had a medium to large effect. To really get the most out of ER, a teacher has a lot to do before, during, and after. Jeon & Day (2015) suggest that there can be "great variation of outcomes depending on the teachers' effort" (p. 306).

DEVELOPMENT

Differences in age, language background and learning environment did not seem to significantly change the order of learning in this study.

———————

Fathman, 1975, p. 42

This study compared 60 Korean and 60 Spanish speakers who were learning English and who were 6-14 years old. Students from two different school programs were also compared, 26 receiving ESL instruction and 18 not in an ESL class.

Recall that language use in this type of research is assessed with spontaneous and unrehearsed oral tasks. In this case, the task was the Second Language Oral Production English (SLOPE) Test, which Fathman created. For example, participants are shown a picture in which the top half is of a ball and are told "Here is a ball." Then, pointing at the bottom half of the page containing a picture of two balls, participants are told "Here are two ____" and the participants orally fill in the blank.

The SLOPE Test is similar to the famous and fun "Wug Test" created by Berko Gleason in 1958. The difference is that the SLOPE Test was created for L2 speakers and uses real words, while the Wug Test was created for L1 speakers and uses nonsense words.

In the "Wug Test," participants are shown a picture of a made-up animal or of a person doing some made-up action and are then prompted to orally fill in the blank in a sentence requiring a different ending on this made-up word. For example, shown a picture in which the top half contains one blue, bird-like creature, the interviewer says, "This is a wug." Then, pointing at the bottom half of the picture illustrating two of these creatures, the interviewer says, "Now there is another one. There are two of them. There are two _____."

Children and adults can instantly apply word-ending patterns to words they have never been exposed to before, which provides evidence of an implicit linguistic system.

DUAL SYSTEMS

... it is logical to believe that oversimplified pedagogical rules taught to L2 learners form a system of linguistic knowledge that they use to monitor their output and, thus, affects their performance. The fact that not even one naturalistic learner demonstrated the observed pattern of target-deviancy that the vast majority of tutored learners did is explained by the fact that they, not having received pedagogical instruction, have no such system of learned linguistic rules of explicit comparisons to their L1, English.

Rothman, 2008, p. 98-99

In this study, highly advanced Spanish L2 speakers who had taken 5 years of language classes and currently teaching Spanish misused preterit and imperfect forms that could be attributed to textbook rules that were inaccurate generalizations. Highly advanced L2 speakers with no classroom experience performed like native speakers. Rothman proposed that even when learners do reach the final stage of native-like knowledge, textbook rule knowledge can override it and lead to target language deviations when the two do not coincide. Called the "Competing Systems Hypothesis," this is a newer formulation of Felix's (1985) "Competition Model."

COMMUNICATION

This [intuition] was that the development of competence in a second language requires not systematization of language inputs or maximization of planned practice, but rather the creation of conditions in which learners engage in an effort to cope with communication.

———————

Prabhu, 1987, p. 1

BELIEFS

Perhaps the most interesting - and most disturbing - argument found in the literature is that because students want correction and believe it is helpful, we should continue the practice... The obligation teachers have to students is not to use whatever form of instruction the students think is best, but rather to help them learn... When students hold a demonstrably false belief about learning, the proper response is not to encourage that belief, but to show them that it is false.

Truscott, 1996, p. 359

Truscott (1999) asks, "How much of students' false faith in correction is due to the reinforcement it receives from their teachers?" (p. 116).

Week 21

READING

. . . (a) when the material being read is relatively easy, then close to 0% of the words will be unknown; (b) when the material is relatively hard, then around 2% or more of the words will be unknown; and (c) when the difficulty level of the material is approximately equal to the ability level of the individual, then around 1% of the words will be unknown.

Carver, 1994, p. 432

In this study, elementary-aged readers and graduate student readers underlined the number of unknown words from texts evaluated to be easy, appropriate, and difficult. This quote summarizes the results. Oh, and one more thing. . . they were reading in their *first* language.

DEVELOPMENT

The results of this study support the claim that the classroom and naturalistic L2 acquisition of complex grammatical features such as word order follow similar routes.

R. Ellis, 1989, p. 305

In this study, instruction did not alter developmental stages. Recall that language use in this type of research is assessed with spontaneous and unrehearsed oral tasks. In this case, the task was a storytelling activity.

TEXTBOOK GRAMMAR

In short, I am suggesting that explicit processes may be engaged as learners employ conscious strategies about what something means, but they do not engage explicit processes in the acquisition of formal properties of language.

———————

VanPatten, 2015a, p. 103

In other words, acquiring abstract features and creating networks of form-meaning connections all happen outside of our awareness. The only thing we are ever directly conscious of are the sounds and appearance of written words (Sharwood Smith & Truscott, 2014b).

Have you wondered whether explicit information (EI) about language can aid comprehension? The classic processing instruction treatment began with EI, provided in layperson terms, about a single target form (rather than presenting the entire paradigm). This was followed by a brief and non-technical explanation of a faulty processing strategy. Subsequent research found that the structured input activities without EI were necessary and sufficient to correct faulty processing strategies (e.g., VanPatten & Oikkenon, 1996). More recent research found that EI only made the intervention more efficient if the information was simple enough that learners could carry it around in their heads, i.e., it was portable (e.g., VanPatten, Borst, Collopy, Qualin, & Price, 2013). Even so, EI was unnecessary to achieve accurate processing.

VOCABULARY

... the three most widely used [German] textbooks do not teach 36–47% of the most frequent 1,000 words... the percentage of vocabulary less frequent than the frequency rank 4,000 is high (29–44%).

———————

Lipinski, 2010, p. 170, 173

Based on a survey of US university German programs, the three leading, first-year textbooks were chosen and the end-of-chapter vocabulary lists were compared to a German frequency dictionary (Jones & Tschirner, 2006). Godev (2009) found similar results when analyzing samples from five popular, first-year Spanish textbooks: only 23-30% of the words were within the most frequent 1,000 words and 13-38% of the words were beyond the most frequent 5,000 words. Only one of the textbooks in the Lipinski analysis said anything about word frequency. The preface said it had been revised by looking at a frequency dictionary (in fact, the same one used in the study). However, the word selection in the textbook that was claiming to be frequency-based turned out to be the least based on frequency of the three textbooks.

BELIEFS

Indeed, the predicament of the modern language teaching profession is that academic credit is earned and diplomas are awarded for the acquisition of skills that, in many cases, are not so well developed as those of a 10-year-old child.

Savignon, 1997, p. 57

In fact, it may very well be that classroom-only learners would be lucky to have developed a mental grammar on par with that of a 3-4-year-old. This is a good reminder that language acquisition is not academic, at least not in the sense that it requires cognitive maturity and critical thinking.

Week 22

READING

… as good pedagogy dictates that when vocabulary knowledge is limited, reading material must be selected that matches these limited lexical resources. It does not make much sense having students read texts for which they do not know 10% or more of the words. Even learners with very small vocabulary sizes can successfully read in an L2 if the reading level is appropriate (e.g., low-level graded readers).

———

Schmitt, Jiang, & Grabe, 2011, p. 36

The English language learners in this study with knowledge of 98% of the words in the texts averaged a 68.3% comprehension score, which was a 10% drop from the average comprehension of learners who knew all of the words in the texts. Based on a few studies that found similar results, it gets recommended that readers know 98% or more of the words in texts during independent reading.

OUTPUT

A look at the data, however, shows that even this weak claim [output sometimes facilitates SLA under some conditions] is hard to support.

Krashen, 1998, p. 175

Krashen argues that research has not demonstrated a direct role for output (e.g., learners can acquire without output) but that doesn't mean he is against output. Krashen has for a long time recognized an indirect and positive role of output (e.g., 1982, p. 60-61). It affects the quantity and quality of the input directed at the learner (e.g., leads to more personalized and comprehensible input, helps you identify as a speaker of the second language, etc.). Thus, the ideal comprehension-based approach does not have students only listening and reading.

An additional consideration in teaching has to be the affective consequences of classroom practices. In the same 1998 article, Krashen points out that speaking activities, especially when done in front of the class, are reported as highly anxiety-provoking (e.g., Young, 1990). That is more likely if the class focuses on accuracy, because then the perceived risk of participation is double, i.e. content *and* form can be wrong. Hence why expectations of output (informed by research on SLA development) have to be level-appropriate.

DUAL SYSTEMS

... the acquisition of metalinguistic knowledge is tied to (conscious) noticing; development of competence is not.

Truscott, 1998, p. 124

(Linguistic) competence is another term for mental grammar. Alternative terms include mental representation and implicit linguistic system.

Competence has traditionally been contrasted with "performance," which refers to language behavior, i.e., use of the language system (Chomsky, 1965). Language use is only an indirect look at what we know (i.e., our mental grammar) and may be influenced by performance problems caused by memory limits, distractions, nervousness, tiredness, boredom, etc.

COMMUNICATIVE TESTS

If communication is the goal, then it is the overall ability to communicate, not grammatical accuracy, which must be tested. This is not easy to do, of course; but to resort to grading based on grammatical accuracy is to avoid our responsibilities. Judgments of fluency will in many cases be subjective; however, if we cannot make those judgments with a reasonable degree of accuracy, then our title as teacher of a second language means very little.

———————

Terrell, 1977, p. 335

One way to do this is to assign global ratings (also called holistic or impressionistic ratings). This can be done with a rating scale (e.g., 1-4) of overall ability. Or break that down into two ratings, fluency (in the temporal sense) and comprehensibility (how easy it is to comprehend the learner). In fact, fluency and comprehensibility ratings were among the main criteria used to evaluate proficiency in Savignon's 1972 study, which has been cited as the start to the communicative movement in language testing (e.g., Brown, 1996).

PRINCIPLES

When the primary goal of second-language teaching is the development of functional oral skills, the prescribed method employs the second language as the medium of instruction; that is, as a vehicle to convey meaning.

Musumeci, 2009, p. 61

Week 23

MENTAL GRAMMAR

The way language works, then, is that each person's brain contains a lexicon of words and the concepts they stand for (a mental dictionary) and a set of rules that combine the words to convey relationships among concepts (a mental grammar).

———————

Pinker, 1994, p. 85

This characterizes the mainstream linguistic perspective. And just to be clear, the lexicon includes much more than the meanings of words. And the "rules" mentioned here are those of a mental grammar, not a textbook grammar. An alternative perspective (e.g., Jackendoff, 2002) does not distinguish words and rules as separate components, instead viewing language as a trio or chain of structures (sound, word order, and meaning) that are activated together during language use.

OUTPUT

... this paper is somewhat speculative, attempting to outline the 'output hypothesis' as I see it at this stage of its development, and provide evidence for it... What measures will be convincing of learning having occurred and what length of time needs to pass between the learning event and the measurement of it, are highly contentious issues in our field. I am convinced by these data that highly specific language learning has taken place. Others will be less convinced.

———————

Swain, 1995, p 125 & 140

The output hypothesis is frequently name-dropped in teacher methodology books as justification for getting students to talk, but what is missing is a critical evaluation of the hypothesis. It would be good to recall the origin of the hypothesis and what data it was originally based upon (see p. 18), in addition to considering later evidence. Some hypotheses in SLA have a greater quantity and quality of support than others, which is to say that not all hypotheses are created equal.

TEXTBOOK GRAMMAR

Despite their label [free-response tests], students who take such tests, I conclude, are indeed focused on form, thanks to the treatment, other measures, and the nature of the tests themselves.

Krashen, 2003, p. 58

Krashen has long argued that participants figure out ". . . that the name of the game was accurate performance on certain structures" (p. 45) and then try to apply consciously learned rules on the tests (i.e., use the "Monitor"). It is a sort of "Hawthorne effect" or "observer's paradox" (Labov, 1972), because when the learners know what the researcher wants, then they may behave differently than they otherwise would. Sociolinguists have tried to diminish the effect of the observer's paradox and get participants to focus on content rather than form by interviewing participants about high-interest topics, using game-like tasks, group interviews, etc.

Krashen considers time to be one of the three conditions for Monitor use, so he is critical of free-response tests that are not time-pressured. However, even time pressure does not rule out the possibility, at least in principle, that learners have gotten fast at using textbook rules. Researchers interested in mental grammar would ideally rule out the possibility that language use is coming from knowledge of textbook grammar. That's why subtle and complex properties that are not taught and unlikely to be figured out are often the focus of research.

COMMUNICATIVE TESTS

Although test evaluation procedures may vary, in real-life communication it is, of course, always the general impression that prevails.

Savignon, 1997, p. 227

Impressionistic rating is more ecologically valid, meaning that it better reflects what we actually do when we communicate: react to overall intelligibility. Not only does this get at the heart of communicative goals, but it's quick and easy. In the words of pronunciation researchers, Derwing and Munro (2009), ". . . judgment data are the gold standard; what listeners perceive is ultimately what matters most" (p. 478). In their research, they have also found that different judges give similar ratings (i.e., reliability is high).

PRINCIPLES

Well-designed programs need to draw on frequency information and also need to have the flexibility for teachers and learners to play a part in choosing the vocabulary to focus on.

Nation, 2013, p. 144

Week 24

MENTAL GRAMMAR

A noun, for example, is simply a word that does nouny things; it is the kind of word that comes after an article, can have an 's stuck onto it, and so on.

———————

Pinker, 1994, p. 106

I recommend reading the first two chapters or so of an introductory linguistics text (e.g., Carnie, 2013), which will demonstrate the complexity of language that we take for granted, as well as reveal how some of the most basic concepts that we learned in school are wrong, e.g., the definitions of parts of speech. To take an example from Carnie (2013), you can identify the nouns in the sentence "The yinkish dripner blorked quastofically into the nindin with the pidibs" (p. 46) without knowing what the words mean. So, what is a noun?

CORRECTION

In other words, teachers can help students' accuracy at least as much by doing nothing as by correcting their grammar; and by doing nothing teachers can avoid the harmful effects discussed above [e.g., raising anxiety, lowering confidence, students simplifying their writing to avoid corrections, and not finding better uses of student and teacher time]. So the alternative to correcting grammar is straightforward: Do not correct grammar.

Truscott, 1996, p. 360-361

Even were it found that acquisition benefitted from correction, additional teaching considerations include a cost-benefit analysis (is it an efficient use of time?) and the affective consequences (e.g., effects on attitude and participation).

TEXTBOOK GRAMMAR

The validity of PI [pronunciation instruction] research both in individual studies and in the aggregate is threatened by the use of very small samples... Three features of PI designs are in need of improvement. First, only 14 percent of the sample examined the longevity of effects by means of a delayed posttest... Secondly, pre-post designs far outnumbered controlled experiments... Third, PI research relies too heavily - primarily even - on controlled outcome measures...

———————

Lee, Jang, & Plonsky, 2015, p. 362-363

This comes from a meta-analysis (including 86 studies) of second language pronunciation instruction. Overall, there was a medium to large effect of instruction, but that effect is not without some serious qualifications.

COMMUNICATION

Our research shows that after 630 to 720 hours of instruction, or about midway through the fourth year of study, approximately 14% of students can read at the Intermediate-Mid level or better. Approximately 16% can write and 6% can speak at this level.

———————

Center for Applied Second Language Studies, 2010, p. 2

Most students in U.S. programs [K-15] do not reach proficiency levels that allow them to effectively communicate in the language.

———————

Center for Applied Second Language Studies, 2011, p. 2

These are the results from 7,515 high school students in their 4th year of Spanish and French programs from 117 schools in 56 districts and 21 states. Proficiency was measured with the Standards-based Measurement of Proficiency (STAMP), an online assessment that uses an evaluation scale based on ACTFL's Proficiency Guidelines (Swender, Conrad, & Vicars, 2012).

Intermediate-Mid is often the proficiency goal of world language programs, because speakers at this level "are able to handle successfully a variety of uncomplicated communicative tasks in straightforward social situations" (Swender, Conrad, & Vicars, 2012, p. 7).

This is essentially a report on the level of communicative ability developed in programs that focus on textbook grammar given the near ubiquity of such instruction. Rule-based instruction has been the status quo in schools for a long time, despite centuries-old, contrary recommendations from language education reformers and a substantial body of research that questions its utility and effectiveness. This reminds me of one of the paradoxes described by Huberman, specialist on educational reform. "That there is no necessary relationship between the proven success of an innovation - even in terms of increments in pupils' achievement or capacities - and its longevity" (Huberman, 1992, p. 6).

Access to the ACTFL Oral Proficiency Interview (OPI) Tester Tutorials is free at www.actfltraining.org (login: actflrater, password: training). There you will see that the intermediate level of proficiency is characterized as the "Survivor" level. OPI ratings reflect the level sustained across all topics discussed during the interview. See Herman (2017) for an overview and critical evaluation of the ACTFL Proficiency Guidelines, including common teacher misunderstandings (e.g., expecting linear progress). Some misunderstandings find clarification in the following statement from the General Preface to the ACTFL

Proficiency Guidelines, a description of Advanced Low speech, and a comment from the OPI tester certification information packet on the proper use of the ACTFL ratings.

The Guidelines are not based on any particular theory, pedagogical method, or educational curriculum. They neither describe how an individual learns a language nor prescribe how an individual should learn a language, and they should not be used for such purposes.

———

Swender, Conrad, & Vicars, 2012, p. 3

Advanced Low speech is typically marked by a certain grammatical roughness (e.g., inconsistent control of verb endings)...

———

Swender, Conrad, & Vicars, 2012, p. 6

Ratings given on the ACTFL scale are intended to be used in conjunction with the ACTFL Oral Proficiency Interview (OPI). ACTFL does not sanction the use of these ratings with other testing instruments.

———

ACTFL, 2018, p. 4

PRINCIPLES

At their very best, the tasks that appear on a test should resemble the kinds of tasks at which learners should be working in the classroom.

———————

Savignon, 1997, p. 241

This is another way of saying "test/assess how you teach, and teach the way in which students will be tested/assessed" (VanPatten, 2017, p. 334). By aligning tests and teaching, the tests are no longer time away from what you want to be doing, i.e., learning. The effect of tests will washback onto when, how, and what gets taught, which is one of Swain's (1984) principles of communicative language testing, i.e., "Work for washback." Tests are also a strong message to our learners about what is important. For instance, if I wanted to encourage more comprehension-based teaching activities, then I would make tests dependent upon (but not necessarily limited to) comprehension, e.g., read a story and then compare/contrast yourself with the character(s). Swain's other three principles are 1) start from somewhere (e.g., base tests on a definition of proficiency), 2) concentrate on content (e.g., use interesting materials that include new information), 3) bias for best (e.g., use level-appropriate tasks).

Week 25

MENTAL GRAMMAR

Finally, the preoccupation of socio-cultural SLL [second language learning] theorists with classroom learning should be noted... This ensures that socio-cultural theory will receive continuing attention, despite its apparent 'incommensurability' with the vision of language as an autonomous and abstract system acquired through specialized mechanisms, which predominates in SLL research and has inspired most of the empirical work . reviewed in this book.

Mitchell & Myles, 2004, p. 222

A linguistic perspective on SLA (a dominant perspective in the field) focuses on mental grammar, which is characterized as abstract, complex, and implicit. This perspective takes a modular view of the mind in which language, like other mental systems (e.g., vision), operates according to its own special set of principles and only responds to a special type of information (i.e., input).

On the contrary, Sociocultural Theory (like Skill Acquisition Theory) focuses on learning that happens inside a classroom, specifically, learning and using explicit knowledge of a textbook grammar. It is a general learning theory (treats SLA like the learning of other subject matters) and, as such, is often familiar to those with a background in general education.

You can see the influence of SCT on popular teacher resources and the practices recommended by some world language organizations. SCT promotes concept-based instruction and ACTFL refers to "teaching grammar as concept" as a guiding principle and a core practice ("Teach grammar as concepts," n.d.). Glisan, 2010 ACTFL president, is coauthor of a popular book that states, "*Teacher's Handbook* supports a sociocultural view of language instruction" (Shrum & Glisan, 2016, p. 36). Chapter 7 of that book promotes the PACE Model (Donato & Adair-Hauck, 1994), which is an application of SCT to the teaching of textbook rules. In PACE, learners are given some context and then figure out the rules by talking with the teacher. These conversations about grammar are referred to as a "dialogic approach." The 2017 book by Glisan and Donato on "high-leverage teaching practices" appears to have reworded ACTFL's guiding principle to "Focusing on form in a dialogic context through PACE."

CORRECTION

Try, just for the moment, to forget you are a language teacher and to listen instead as an interested participant.

Savignon, 1976, p. 16

In a similar vein, Lonsdale (2006) contrasted language teachers and parents. Based on his language learning experience and that of other successful language learners, he recommended that learners get a "language parent," which he defined as "someone who will engage you in conversation in the language you are learning, but who will not try to be your teacher" (p. 178). His 4 rules for language parents are that they 1) try hard to comprehend, 2) never correct "errors," 3) provide feedback on what they comprehend, and 4) use words that the learners know (TEDx, 2013).

DUAL SYSTEMS

Thus, explicit instruction of grammar, as is often given in classrooms to L2 learners, should encourage learning in declarative memory (which may then inhibit learning or processing in procedural memory). Conversely, exposure to the L2 without explicit instruction, as often occurs in immersion contexts, might enhance grammar acquisition in procedural memory, and thus lead to more L1-like processing of grammar.

———

Ullman, 2015, p. 142

Ullman is a neuroscientist and the leading proponent of the Declarative-Procedural Model in SLA (not to be confused with Skill Acquisition Theory that uses similar terms). The declarative memory system is the part of the brain where knowledge of facts and events lies. It is the only system underlying explicit knowledge, but also underlies implicit knowledge. The procedural memory system underlies motor and cognitive skills and is implicit. The DP model predicts that both memory systems can simultaneously learn the same knowledge, but that use of knowledge from one system can block learning and use of knowledge in the other system. Initial learning can be faster in declarative memory, but processing in the procedural memory system can eventually be more automatic.

VOCABULARY

... many second-year books consciously focus on contemporary issues like 'saving the environment' or 'fighting against unjust social forces.' As admirable as these attempts may be in terms of preparing students to engage in a particular set of social causes, it apparently has the effect of having them focus on vocabulary that – at least outside of those limited domains – will probably be of little value in speaking and writing Spanish.

Davies & Face, 2006, p. 139

PRINCIPLES

They [students] do not waste time trying to learn to write before they can read, or trying to learn to read before they can understand a discussion of what they are reading. They do not waste time studying artificial materials that present a cramped, impoverished picture of the language, or learning grammar rules of doubtful utility and questionable accuracy. Nor do they waste time worrying about daily quizzes and weekly tests.

———————

Hastings, 2003

This describes the FOCAL SKILLS approach developed for intensive university-level ESL classrooms by Hastings and Wheatley in 1987. The program focuses on one skill at a time (except the last module), progressing from listening to reading to writing to an advanced module. The main activity of the listening module is MovieTalk, in which the teacher plays and pauses a film while narrating, paraphrasing dialogue, and asking short-answer questions to check comprehension. Students in FS programs make about three times the gains in the focal skill and make equal progress in the other skills as compared to standard ESL programs (Hastings, 1995; Yu, 1998).

143

Week 26

The teacher is to control his language in the classroom in the same way that an adult controls his language in conversing with a child. . .

———————

Prabhu, 1987, p. 45

Think about what else a parent does when communicating with a young child, e.g., does a parent require the child to respond in complete sentences? And consider how much trust parents have in the process of language acquisition. To what extent are they "language teachers"?

CORRECTION

… probably no amount of evidence will convince many teachers, students, or researchers that grammar correction is misguided. Thus, it is also necessary to undermine the intuitions, to show that correction does not have to help and in fact should not be expected to help.

———————

Truscott, 1996, p. 341

Truscott identified the core assumption that underlies a pro-grammar correction bias: correction *must* work. From this bias it is claimed that students will fossilize (i.e., stop developing) without correction. There is no evidence that this actually happens. Higgs & Clifford (1982) is commonly cited to support this argument, but the authors were just expressing an opinion based on their own teaching experience.

As Truscott (1996) points out, the core assumption also underlies the "burden of proof assumption" that says that as long as there is any possibility that it helps, teachers should

145

keep correcting grammar. The problem is that this position is unfalsifiable, because there could always be some version of correction that has yet to be tested. And the alternative, that we don't correct until there is evidence of its effectiveness, is just as logical (if not more so, given the time-consuming nature of the practice).

The core assumption and burden of proof assumption motivate much of Ferris's (1999) response to Truscott in which she defends written grammar correction. Ferris says the current research evidence is "scarce" (p. 8), "limited, dated, incomplete, and inconclusive" (p. 9), and "inadequate" (p. 10). In other words, she continues to support grammar correction even though it has no research basis, or worse, she thinks that no research evidence is needed to justify the continuation of this practice, because personal experience and intuition are sufficient. See Truscott (1999) for his response to Ferris.

TEXTBOOK GRAMMAR

Proceduralizing and (at least partially) automatizing such distinctions [features in the L2 that don't exist in the L1] takes a very large amount of practice... Of course no degree of teaching and practice in the classroom will lead to 'perfect' knowledge of the language; it would be utterly naïve to expect that, given that even many years of residence in the target environment do not.

———————

DeKeyser, 2010, p. 158

In defense of rule-based instruction, you sometimes hear "Implicit learning takes more time than what we have in schools." There are at least three major problems with that logic. 1) To implicitly grow a language system to a near-native level takes a lot of time, but it takes much less time to develop conversational fluency. 2) When you engage in a different process from first language acquisition, then the result is a qualitatively different type of product. In other words, there are no shortcuts to native-type knowledge. 3) As stated in the quote, this other (skill-building) process takes a long time, too. Then, there are classrooms that try to develop both the core language system and metalinguistic knowledge, the latter purportedly beneficial for writing accuracy. But if each of these processes takes time, then can we have our cake and eat it, too?

147

COMMUNICATION

Languages are learned not as forming in themselves a part of erudition or wisdom, but as being the means by which we may acquire knowledge and may impart it to others.

———————

Comenius, 1657, p. 203

... [students] should learn, and learn thoroughly, the etymology of all words, the reasons for all constructions, and the principles on which the rules for the various subjects of study have been formed.

———————

Comenius, 1657, p. 154

Comenius's communicative-based philosophy (e.g., language as medium) conflicted with his rule-based recommendations (e.g., language as object) for classroom practice.

BELIEFS

... the value of statutory implementation as a means of bringing about better learning in a large number of classrooms is questionable generally... because the quality of teaching in any classroom is dependent on the teacher's pedagogic perception, quite apart from his or her abilities and the teaching conditions.

———————

Prabhu, 1987, p. 105

Week 27

For learners of English with a vocabulary of less than 2,000 words, most unsimplified text is just too difficult and does not provide the conditions necessary for learning through meaning-focused input.

———————

Nation, 2013, p. 229

2,000 words is probably an underestimate. Nation (2006) found that for ungraded written texts, a vocabulary size of 4,000 word families was needed in order to know 95% of the words. Knowledge of 8,000-9,000 word families provided coverage of 98% of the words.

For ungraded conversation, a vocabulary size of 3,000 word families corresponded to knowledge of 95% of the words and 6,000-7,000 word families provided 98% coverage.

DEVELOPMENT

One important observation of this study is that there was relatively little improvement over time in the accuracy of learners' use of the six grammatical morphemes in obligatory contexts even though grammatical accuracy was always the focus of their ESL classes.

Lightbown, 1983, p. 240

In this one-year, longitudinal study, rules that were taught and drilled were overused, i.e., used in the wrong contexts. As Lightbown (1983) wrote of the mechanical drill practice (e.g., conjugation exercises), ". . . we may be setting up barriers which have to be broken down before the learners can begin to build up their own interlanguage systems" (p. 239). Essentially, that means that this type of instruction was delaying acquisition. There was also no relationship found in this study between input frequency and output accuracy. Recall that language use in this type of research is assessed with spontaneous and unrehearsed oral tasks. In this case, the task was a picture-based card game.

TEXTBOOK GRAMMAR

Yet, these non-beginners did not show evidence of any mental representation for the very thing that has been present in their formal instruction from the first day of Spanish classes. . . A singular question comes to mind from the viewpoint of the current volume, 'What happened to all that instruction, practice, feedback, and so on related to person-number endings in Spanish? Where did it go?'

———————

VanPatten & Rothman, 2014, p. 15-16

This refers to the finding from a self-paced reading study (VanPatten, Keating, & Leeser; 2012) in which third year university Spanish students, unlike native speakers, did not slow down when they read sentences with incorrect present tense verb endings. However, learners did show sensitivity to some word order violations that had never been taught.

ENJOYMENT

Theoretically, the essence of the method [Shared Book Experience] is that new learning takes place at the point of interest, rather than in accordance with a carefully graded linguistic pattern.

———————

Elley & Mangubhai, 1983, p. 58

Stories are one possible organizing unit for a communicative syllabus, in which case the communicative purpose is to learn new information and to be entertained. Such a program design can be referred to as story-based.

PRINCIPLES

More systematic activities are needed; this does not mean repetitive manipulation of form, but can take a variety of shapes, from initial communicative drills to role-playing activities, task-based learning, and content-based teaching.

———————

DeKeyser, 2010, p. 162

You will recall that Skill Acquisition Theory (SAT) focuses on the development of metalinguistic fluency. Remarkably, different theories of SLA converge on what is best teaching practice. Van den Branden's chapter in DeKeyser's 2007 book on SAT identified 3 key conditions for classrooms: 1) interactional support, 2) meaningful and relevant tasks, and 3) a positive, safe climate.

Week 28

COMPREHENSION

Current comprehension tests – the Nelson Danny, the comprehension subtest of the SAT and the like – were developed with a psychometric rationale and do not reflect our understanding of comprehension processes (for further discussion, see Shepard, 2000). There is no uniform comprehension process to be measured. Instead, comprehension involves different levels and a variety of skills. . .

———

Kintsch & Kintsch, 2005, p. 62

Without a clear understanding of what comprehension is, how can we assess it? Generally speaking, "What?" questions (e.g., "What did the character do?") test the textbase level and "Why?" questions (e.g., "Why did the character do that?") test the situation model level. Many beginner-level L2 comprehension tests only require knowledge of a few key words, are based on low-frequency textbook vocabulary, and/or test how readers cope with texts beyond their level (i.e., strategic competence).

DEVELOPMENT

... different conditions of exposure to English L2 do not significantly alter the accuracy order in which grammatical morphemes are produced.

———————

Pica, 1983, p. 465

In this study, the adult learners had similar accuracy orders as children acquiring a second language. This was true regardless of whether the learners were only exposed to the second language in the classroom, only outside of the classroom, or had had a mix of classroom and non-classroom experiences.

The classroom-only learners overused rules. The non-classroom learners relied on premodifying quantifiers (e.g., *many, few, etc.*) more than the other groups in instances where learners should have expressed a plural noun (e.g., *three boy*). However, the non-classroom learners may have left out the final -s, even though they knew it should be there. The classroom-only learners were from Mexico City where final consonants tend to be pronounced, while the non-classroom learners may have mostly been from the Caribbean where the final -s tends to be dropped (VanPatten, 1988).

Recall that language use in this type of research is assessed with spontaneous and unrehearsed oral tasks. In this case, the task was an hour-long conversation with an interviewer about familiar topics.

TEXTBOOK GRAMMAR

Whereas the early instructed SLA did not operationalize the instructional treatment in any way, the current state of affairs is that L2 instruction is typically designed and measured in ways that are not psycholinguistically valid. In other words, processing in which learners typically engage in instructed SLA research to date is not of the kind relevant to SLA processes.

Doughty, 2004, p. 193

Doughty states as fact that textbook grammar instruction is irrelevant to the development of a mental grammar. She recommended a framework for designing and analyzing instructed SLA studies and part of the first phase is to exclude metalinguistic treatments, because "the one type of process that is known not to be relevant to SLA are culled early on" (p. 195).

ENJOYMENT

... starting with comprehension, the gift of talking will eventually appear – and the process of language acquisition, from beginning to end, will be intrinsically pleasurable.

———————

Asher, 1981, p. 220

Asher invented the Total Physical Response method in which the students act out what the teacher says.

PRINCIPLES

… eclecticism at the classroom level invariably degenerates into an unsystematic, unprincipled, and uncritical pedagogy because teachers with very little professional preparation to be eclectic in a principled way have little option but to randomly put together a package of techniques from various methods and label it eclectic.

———————

Kumaravadivelu, 1994, p. 30

Week 29

MENTAL GRAMMAR

... language learning involves considerable unconscious "tallying" (Ellis, 2002a) of construction frequencies, and language use requires exploitation of this implicit statistical knowledge (Bod, Hay, & Jannedy, 2003; Bybee & Hopper, 2001; Chater & Manning, 2006).

Despite that many of us go to great lengths to engage in explicit language learning, the bulk of language acquisition is implicit learning from usage. Most knowledge is tacit knowledge; most learning is implicit; the vast majority of our cognitive processing is unconscious.

———

N. Ellis, 2009, p. 145

———

N. Ellis & Wulff, 2015, p. 89

After Universal Grammar (UG), usage-based approaches make up the next major contemporary perspective on SLA, of which Nick C. Ellis is a leading proponent. Usage-based approaches reject any innate structures, instead positing that what is innate is the capacity to learn language. The same mechanisms used in general learning are used to unconsciously connect language items and, largely based on frequency of input processing, calculate the statistical probability of them occurring together. Like UG, usage-based approaches depend on input to develop a mental grammar.

What is learned are called "constructions," which are form-meaning and form-function pairings that exist at all levels of language. They range from the simple link between an individual word and its meaning to the link between a passive construction and its function (i.e., taking the focus off of the doer of the action). There are no "rules" of grammar. Underlying rule-like behavior are vastly interconnected networks of form and meaning/function connections. First and second languages are also interconnected and simultaneously activated such that you cannot turn off a language.

Usage-based approaches are a relative newcomer in SLA. The major motivation of UG is one of the major challenges to this approach: how to explain the logical problem (i.e., learners know more than what they are exposed to in the input). However, the two frameworks can be complementary, so long as they are explaining different phenomena (e.g., verb endings vs. word order). After all, UG explains what is common to all languages, but every language has its own word forms that must be linked to meaning/function and stored.

DEVELOPMENT

Language learning perceived in this way cannot be specifically predicted or controlled by language teaching.

———————

Prabhu, 1987, p. 71

This pedagogical principle was arrived at after a discussion of how language learning happens outside of conscious awareness, the learner acquiring different aspects of language at different rates, all while the learner focuses on meaning. Prabhu noted that his perception of language learning overlapped considerably with findings from second language acquisition research, but "for the most part developed independently, and in the context of an exploration of language teaching rather than directly of language learning" (p. 69). Related to Prabhu's idea, research has found that developmental patterns are not altered by instruction. This quote is also the practical implication of having a class of learners at different places in their interlanguage development and not knowing the state of every learner's interlanguage.

TEXTBOOK GRAMMAR

Thus overall, the evidence indeed seems to suggest that although explicit training can provide fast early grammar learning, it might slow the attainment of native-like grammatical processing and possibly native-like proficiency as well... If the learner's goal is rapid learning rather than the eventual attainment of high proficiency, explicit training might do the trick. But if native-like attainment is desired, explicit training might be harmful, and it might be better to stick solely or largely with more implicit training approaches, such as immersion.

———————

Morgan-Short, Finger, Grey, & Ullman, 2012, p. 15

COMMUNICATION

In light of the historical record, the definition of what is 'traditional' language teaching becomes impossibly difficult to establish.

———————

Musumeci, 2009, p. 46

Besides rule-based instruction, content-based instruction (i.e., immersion schooling) also has a long history. The real tradition is the simultaneous prescription of communicative language teaching and the institutionalization of rule-based practice, i.e. theory is not realized in practice.

PRINCIPLES

A group of teachers holding similar beliefs about language and language learning (i.e., sharing a similar approach) may each implement these principles in different ways.

———————

Richards & Rodgers, 2014, p. 29

Teachers may share similar principles, but have to be experts of their context (i.e., the students and the setting) in order to determine how to best apply them. Thus, the design and procedures of a classroom will vary based on context, although the pedagogical principles based on SLA research may be the same. If method encompasses principles, design, and procedures (see p. 63), then in this case, method will vary, but principles will not.

Week 30

If learners spent time learning the low-frequency words in a text without vocabulary control, this learning would be largely wasted because it would be a long time before they had a chance to meet or use these words again.

———————

Nation, 2013, p. 224

DEVELOPMENT

The review of research on the effect of instruction on SL development suggests the following conclusions. First, formal SL instruction does not seem able to alter acquisition sequences, except temporarily and in trivial ways which may even hinder subsequent development. On the other hand, instruction has what are possibly positive effects on SLA processes, clearly positive effects on the rate at which learners acquire the language, and probably beneficial effects on their ultimate level of attainment.

Larsen-Freeman & Long, 1991, p. 321

How does this jive with the concept of teaching for mastery? What can a teacher control? To what type of instruction or aspect of instruction are we to attribute the positive effects on the rate of acquisition?

TEXTBOOK GRAMMAR

Teaching practices that rely on transfer of knowledge, without any concern for the processes underlying the development of the language system, are not promising.

Truscott, 1996, p. 343

COMMUNICATION

The problem is that many activities introduced as communicative are not communicative at all but structure drills in disguise. Grammar often remains the hidden agenda.

———————

Savignon, 1997, p. 202

PRINCIPLES

The effective language teacher is someone who can provide input and help make it comprehensible in a low anxiety situation. Of course, many teachers have felt this way about their task for years, at least until they were told otherwise by the experts!

———————

Krashen, 1982, p. 32

If you have read through this entire book, then you are well on your way to becoming the expert on language learning that your students need. And after reading what has been written by dozens of experts on second language acquisition, it should be clear that those are not the "experts" referred to in the current quote.

Conclusion

If curiosity got the best of you and you skipped to the conclusion, then please read the rest of this paragraph before deciding to continue on. The perspective expressed below is a synthesis (and sometimes repetition) of all that came before it. Without the requisite background knowledge, the conclusion may be less accessible. Depending on your background in second language acquisition (SLA), this could be a lot to take in at once, intellectually and emotionally speaking. Some commonly held beliefs about language learning will be challenged. I do not want to turn you away before you have had the chance to read through the quotes and commentary. So, only read on if you can keep an open mind and may any doubt and disagreement inspire you to seek answers from within this text and beyond. Come back to the conclusion after you complete the thirty weeks and see how your view has been reinforced and/or changed.

Before you read my response, you ought to consider how you would answer the question: How do you acquire a second language? You can break that into two separate, but related questions: What do you acquire? How do you acquire? Did vocabulary and grammar come to mind when thinking about the "what"? If so, are you thinking of the word lists and rules in textbooks? How is that the same or different from the mental dictionary and mental grammar that linguists study? And when you considered the "how" of acquisition, did you think of things like input, output, rules, practice, and correction? If so, how do input, output, and the rest get "turned into" the "what" that ends up in our heads? Take a moment to jot down your own thoughts.

I preface my response by saying that I am not committed to this being *the* answer. It is based on the information in this text, but that doesn't mean I am not open to changing my view. I also want to make clear that nothing I write is an idea that originates with me. I am summarizing a mainstream perspective shared by many contemporary SLA researchers.

Part 1: How do you acquire a second language?

At the heart of any answer is the following question: To what extent are the processes and mechanisms that underlie first language acquisition the same as those of second language acquisition?

My answer is a dual systems approach in which learners can draw on at least two different sources of knowledge to interpret and express messages. Since the beginning of the second language acquisition (SLA) field in the 1970s (e.g., Krashen, 1975), there has existed a dual systems model (i.e., the Monitor Model). A version of this model is still alive and well today, albeit refined, elaborated, and dressed in contemporary terminology (e.g., Rothman, 2008; Schwartz, 1993; Sharwood Smith & Truscott, 2014b).

There are multiple theories of SLA (for review, see, e.g., VanPatten & Williams, 2015), but really, some of these theories are not in competition, because they are not trying to describe the development of the same type of knowledge. To construct a native type of knowledge, mental properties and capacities that we are born with act on the language that we try to comprehend. A distinct type of knowledge that is not made of the same stuff as native-like knowledge develops from learning and practicing textbook rules. Despite the appeal of "you can teach it however you want," engaging different processes does not result in the same product in our heads.

Before I go any further, some key terms, and the domain of SLA needs to be defined. The dominant view is that SLA is the study of internal mental states and their changes (Gregg, 2003; cf. Firth & Wagner, 1997). "Language" refers to the properties of the internal language system and the development or growth of that system is what is termed "acquisition."

Any good theory of SLA needs to be able to explain two principal observations (among others): the logical problem (Hornstein & Lightfoot, 1981) and the developmental problem (Felix, 1984). The logical problem asks how it is possible to know more than what learners have been exposed to (this is also known as the poverty of the stimulus). This includes knowing when sentences are ungrammatical, even though we have never heard the sentences before and no one has ever told us that the sentences are ungrammatical. To answer this problem requires a theory of language, the "what" of acquisition. That is what linguists study and it only takes reading the first chapter of an introductory linguistics book to understand that the "rules" in our head bear little to no resemblance to textbook rules.

As for the second major observation, the problem is to explain why learners follow universal stages of acquisition, that is, the "how" of acquisition. There are many different developmental stages and orders that have been documented and that are not altered by instruction (for review, see, e.g., Lightbown & Spada, 2013), which I think is the finding with the greatest implications for teachers. This is also the finding that essentially launched the entire field of SLA about fifty years ago (Dulay & Burt, 1973). Accuracy doesn't develop on the teacher's schedule and teachers get a glimpse of that whenever they ask their students to communicate spontaneously and freely about something they have not rehearsed.

Input is the main, if not exclusive ingredient that connects the "how" of acquisition to the "what." Various definitions of input have been proposed. Sharwood Smith (1993) defined input as "potentially processible language data" (p. 167). Wong and VanPatten (2003) defined it as "communicatively-oriented language that they [learners] hear or see and attend to for meaning" (p. 407). There has been widespread agreement about the causal status of input since the beginning of the scientific study of SLA (e.g., Krashen, 1982; Gregg, 1984; White, 1987), but what is disputed are the details of how the input is used to construct the language system (i.e., mental grammar) and how to characterize that system. Whereas a linguistic perspective posits that we are all born with an inventory of constraints on language and input is needed to choose which of those constraints are relevant in a given language, a psychology-based perspective (i.e., usage-based approaches) proposes that we unconsciously count and associate pieces of language with each other based on the input we are exposed to. All this is not to say that output is not beneficial. However, its role is different. For example, both of the aforementioned perspectives would allow a potential role for output in improving access to and skill at using knowledge that has already been acquired from input.

Now, it sometimes appears that second language acquisition is harder than first language acquisition, and the outcomes *are* more variable than in first language acquisition. From this, it is tempting to conclude that first and second language acquisition are different (see, e.g., Bley-Vroman, 1990; cf. Schwartz, 1990). However, there are many internal, as well as external factors that contribute to these differences, but that do not change the basic internal architecture and underlying process. To name just two factors, there are differences in the quantity and quality of input and obviously, you did not already have another language in your head when you acquired a first language. Does it even make sense to expect a bilingual to obtain the same knowledge as that of a monolingual? After all, a bilingual is not simply two monolinguals in one brain. And then there's another sort of SLA outcome that strongly supports the similarity of first and second language acquisition, that is, evidence of the logical problem. This is the lead motivator of the

176

operation of Universal Grammar (UG) in first and second language acquisition.

Twenty years ago or so, the evidence reached what has been called a "critical mass" (Rothman & Slabakova, 2018, p. 423; for review, see, e.g., White, 2003), because so many studies found the same thing: people have second language knowledge that arguably could not have come from the first language, instruction, learning by analogy, nor even from the input (for an overview, see Schwartz & Sprouse, 2013). That is only deemed possible if we are born with this knowledge and if second language learners can still make use of it in learning and using a second language.

I will provide one brief and simplified example. Imagine I am talking about my family and what you need to know is that all the members of my family are short. If I said in English "Nobody thinks that he is tall," then it can mean that not one person in my family thinks of himself or herself as being tall. You get the same interpretation if you say the sentence in Spanish but do not pronounce the pronoun for "he," which is allowed in Spanish ("Nadie cree que es alto"). But, if I pronounce the pronoun in Spanish, then the interpretation changes and "he" refers to someone else other than a member in my family.

English speakers learning Spanish at beginning, intermediate, and advanced levels know this and the higher the level, the more native-like they are (Peréz-Leroux & Glass, 1999). But this subtle difference is something they could not have learned from their first language, it is not something they were ever taught, and they were never exposed to the sentence with the incorrect interpretation and were told it was wrong. This restriction on pronoun interpretation exists in all languages that allow pronouns not to be pronounced, such as Spanish and Chinese. Everyone is born with this restriction (i.e., the Overt Pronoun Constraint). It is not something that is learned, but only becomes active in second language acquisition when the learner processes input from a language that does not pronounce pronouns.

Each of the subsystems – sound, sentence structure, and meaning – are guided by their own principles. But what about learning new word forms and their meanings? Here is where usage-based approaches provide insight. Words that often occur together, like "good" and "morning" and that overlap in form, like "right" and "fright," or are related in meaning, like "apple" and "banana," are linked. All the links result in intricate webs and the strength of the links is determined by the frequency of input processing.

Turning to the developmental problem, there is ample evidence that SLA is constrained and stage-like, much like first language acquisition. Children and adult second language learners, inside and outside of a classroom, all follow similar output orders and stages (e.g., Bailey, Madden, & Krashen, 1974; R. Ellis, 1989; Pica, 1983). Multiple factors can conspire to create these stages. For one, there are limits on what learners can process in the input. In other words, they filter the input such that not all of it can be used right away in the construction of the acquired systems in their heads (see, e.g., VanPatten, 1996, 2004, 2015b). And two, there are limits on what learners can produce in real time. Learners develop the ability to match up grammatical information within the same phrase, as in the noun phrase "two kids," before they can match up information between phrases, as in subject-verb agreement. In fact, according to this proposed developmental hierarchy, subject-verb agreement is stage five of six total stages and stages cannot be skipped (Pienemann, 1998, 2005).

I will now briefly discuss the other potential source of knowledge: information we have *about* language (i.e., metalinguistic knowledge). The most common form of this knowledge are the rules found in textbooks made for language learners. Textbook rules are distinct from the "rules" (i.e., abstract properties) that characterize a native type of language system and that underlie use of that system. Rather, textbook rules are generalizations made about the products of using a mental grammar. There are two main and competing theories of metalinguistic

179

learning: Skill Acquisition Theory (SAT) and Sociocultural Theory (SCT). In SAT, learners try to learn a rule that they then practice until its use becomes faster and faster. In SCT, the rule is learned first with the help of visuals and other materials, then with the support of others, until it is internalized. Because these two theories do not intend to explain the logical and developmental problems, and because the process and product is qualitatively different from what was discussed prior, these are peripheral theories of SLA, or even considered to fall outside the domain of SLA.

It is up to research to determine the optimal conditions and potential limitations on the use of a textbook grammar. Sometimes you come across comments that explicit instruction, where that gets defined as rule-based instruction, is better than an approach that doesn't teach textbook rules. But there are many "buts" to such a statement, not the least of which is the fact that most studies measure language gains with controlled tests and only measure gains in the short term. Even one lead advocate of SAT acknowledges that the theory best accounts for what happens in 1) high-aptitude, 2) adult, 3) beginner learners, of 4) easy-to-explain rules in 5) a classroom (DeKeyser, 2015). It's also important to recognize that SAT would not support some common grammar teaching practices, because too much time gets spent on exercises that don't require attention to meaning (e.g., conjugation practice) and too much is covered, which means that learners don't spend enough time developing procedural and automatized knowledge. Moreover, neither SAT nor SCT denies that what happens in the minds of learners in non-grammar-oriented contexts is qualitatively different.

Sometimes, the native and the non-native systems are said to compete such that instruction tailored to one system can interfere with learning by the other system (e.g., Felix, 1985; Rothman, 2008; Ullman, 2015). For instance, a brain study found that learners getting only about ten minutes of explicit grammar teaching did not have native-like brain responses, even after they spent three and a half hours on meaning-based comprehension and production practice. The group that was not taught grammar and only got the meaning-based practice did show native-like brain patterns (Morgan-Short, Finger, Grey, & Ullman, 2012).

In summary, on the one hand, second language learners can develop a mental grammar that is qualitatively the same as the first language system in that both consist of constraints and word webs that internal mechanisms activate and construct from interpreting input. That process is called "acquisition." Choosing the language-specific constraints and forming word webs all happen outside of our awareness. The only thing we are ever directly conscious of are the sounds and appearance of written words (e.g., Sharwood Smith & Truscott,

2014b). And we can use intentional problem-solving to aid us in figuring out the meaning of the language we hear or read (VanPatten, 2015c).

On the other hand, with practice, we can develop some ability to use explicit knowledge of textbook rules. This may help (some of us more than others) to communicate under some conditions. However, there are limitations on the learning and use of this knowledge and it may interfere with the development and use of a native-like system.

Whereas forty years ago, the distinction between two different knowledge sources and processes (i.e., "acquisition" versus "learning") was largely a metaphor, today, more of the details have been sketched out and will continue to be filled in by future research.

An earlier draft of part 1 of the conclusion was filmed and can be viewed here: https://youtu.be/0TS71OR_lRE

Part 2: How do you teach a second language?

Learning how second languages are acquired is a prerequisite to determining how to best teach a second language. Language teachers generally agree that the goal is to develop communicative ability and research on second language acquisition can tell us a lot about how to do it. There are two sources of knowledge that potentially contribute to communicative ability. There is one process for developing a textbook grammar and another for developing a mental grammar. So, the first decision a teacher has to make is whether or not the goal is to develop a language system that is qualitatively the same as a first language system (i.e., a mental grammar). One problem (among others) with trying to learn both a textbook grammar and a mental grammar is that each requires a significant time commitment to develop to the point of fluent use. When making this decision, keep in mind the limitations of rule-based instruction, e.g., the chances of success at developing metalinguistic ability are better with "high-aptitude adult learners" (DeKeyser, 2015, p. 101).

If you choose to focus on mental grammar, what I consider an "acquisition-centered classroom," then the implications for pedagogy have long been apparent (e.g., Krashen, 1982). Despite criticisms of the first formulation of a dual systems approach, the pedagogical principles derived of this approach were embraced by many, including many critics. The harshest critic had this to say: "I agree with him [Krashen] that most language learning is unconscious, that comprehensible input is vital for learning and that a teacher's most important job is to provide that input, that affective barriers can prevent successful acquisition of a second language and that a teacher has the duty to try to lower those barriers whenever possible. But then, does anybody disagree?" (Gregg, 1984, p. 94).

Therefore, much of class time ought to be spent on teacher-led, whole-class activities, because the teacher can provide students with a greater quantity and quality of exposure to the language than what they can get from listening to a classmate. Level-appropriate and high-interest input can also come from an extensive reading program that offers students time to select from a variety of books that they read independently. Maximizing comprehension doesn't mean just listening and reading. Interaction is beneficial, because it can make the language spoken by others more comprehensible and can personalize the discussion (e.g., Long, 1981; Pica, Young, & Doughty, 1987).

When the input is provided in a truly communicative context with a truly communicative purpose, then learners will put more effort into comprehension. Thus, the central guiding principle for an acquisition-centered classroom is to maximize comprehension during communicative events. The approach that results is comprehension-based and communicative. This approach is far from new. In fact, major educational reformers of the 15th, 16th, and 17th centuries had similar ideas about how to develop communicative ability (Musumeci, 1997, 2009). But the implementation of this approach in schools has repeatedly been corrupted, largely because it is mistaken as a better way of teaching a textbook grammar.

An alternative approach requires an alternative curriculum. Ideally, the syllabus and assessments enable, support, and encourage classroom practices that are comprehension-based and communicative, rather than restrict those practices. In order to personalize communication and maximize engagement, content and activities need to remain flexible. The nature of second language development means that it is inappropriate to teach for mastery, nor is it appropriate to expect learners to achieve the same outcome at the same point in time. Therefore, a comprehension-based and communicative approach to language teaching demands versatility of classroom activity and expects variable outcomes, which means that syllabi and assessments will have to be designed accordingly. When content is predetermined (as in "forward design") then syllabus coverage takes precedent over the learners' needs and interests. This also occurs, albeit to a lesser degree, when outcomes are predetermined (as in "backwards design"). Rather than a "syllabus first" program, curriculum design for an acquisition-centered program starts with process in order to put the learner first. After all, what matters most for classroom acquisition is what happens during the class period. Therefore, the primary focus is on selecting activities and procedures that create optimal conditions and experiences for learners to acquire a second language. There would be plentiful opportunities for learners to influence the course content and pacing. Richards (2013) termed this curriculum approach "central design." I prefer to call it "forward procedure," because curriculum design starts with procedures and goes forward from there. By doing so, it best enables teachers to start with where students are and choose procedures to give students what they want/need to move forward. I have a feeling that this is what good teachers of any subject matter have always done, but many have had to do it by ignoring the syllabus and tests.

In a forward procedure approach to curriculum design, the content on the syllabus emerges, reactive to student needs and interests. What to teach and when to teach it is not predetermined. This is a characteristic shared by a procedural syllabus (e.g., Prabhu, 1987), process syllabus (e.g., Breen, 1984), and a negotiated syllabus (Clarke, 1991). A teacher may have a plan, but has to be able to adapt it. The syllabus that emerged from the previous year can serve as the tentative plan for the current year. The syllabus would then consist of a list of potential activities and loosely sequenced content. As an example, one way of structuring a syllabus is around a loose collection of stories and story-based activities. The content that makes up a communicative syllabus is not a list of words or rules, but rather, consists of personal information, stories, culture, subject matter, and/or universal themes such as fears, dreams, family and friends, accidents, etc. In fact, the ready-to-adapt syllabus could be a general blueprint for every level of the program. Then, the teacher modifies the activities and content to the interests and proficiency levels of the learners.

Learners will be most engaged when the content and activities are of personal interest and intrigue. I have found that engagement is highest with use of an interactional strategy I like to refer to as "collaborative construction," which consists of the teacher asking questions and using student answers to create something new (e.g., character, scene, dialogue, image, etc.). When used to create stories, this is known as collaborative storytelling, which is the essence of role-playing games and is at the heart of the method called Teaching Proficiency through Reading and Storytelling (Ray & Seely, 2019). With a few high-interest activities and the ability to adjust speech to the level of the learners, then lesson planning becomes really easy. It can be as simple as selecting the story you want to create or the content you want to discuss. Then, the teacher can exert the majority of his/her effort on the moment-by-moment interaction with the learners and on developing the skills necessary to sustain communication with the class.

There needn't be concern that teachers are not covering the same words, because covering is not the same thing as learning. It is inevitable that the breadth and depth of word knowledge will be variable between learners. So, teachers will do what they've always done when a word impedes communication, i.e., translate, gesture, etc. There is even an advantage to students knowing different words, i.e., input from peers is an opportunity for acquisition. Think about how difficult and restraining (if not impossible) it would be if parents had to restrict communication to the next word on a frequency list. By definition, higher frequency words are those that occur more often and across a wider variety of contexts, which means any communicative event will include some of these words. And to maximize comprehension, the teacher has to limit the number of new words, which ensures repetition of higher frequency words. The consequence of this curriculum approach to language teaching is the acquisition of useful language, plus words that come from topics of personal interest, as well as words that are necessary for communication in a classroom context.

If teaching is activity-based and content-based, then communicative assessments would measure how successfully learners completed the activities and/or how well the new content was learned. And again, the content is not the language, but what was learned from communicating in the second language. If you have to use "common assessments" across different class sections, then the question becomes how to still maintain the flexibility in activities and content that this approach demands. The solution is to adopt common task-types and scoring procedures. For example, different classes may be working with different stories or learning different cultural content, but the type of assessment task would be the same across sections, e.g., read a story or biographical text and then compare/contrast yourself with a character. Teachers would agree beforehand how these would be scored, e.g., rate the quality and/or count the quantity of comparisons made. Discrete-type responses (e.g., multiple choice) are also acceptable, because the focus is on information learned, rather than language knowledge and ability.

The assessments can be done in the second language when it doesn't keep students from demonstrating their content knowledge. However, the implication of second language developmental research is that it is inappropriate to expect that everyone will be able to deal with the same level of language use. The rate of acquisition between students is known to be variable and progress is interspersed between periods of plateaus, all of which is outside of the learner's conscious control. Therefore, is it fair to hold everyone to the same outcome-based standard and/or expect everyone to make the same amount of progress? This is a prime example of when fair is not equal and is a serious challenge to product-oriented practices, which includes "backwards design" (in which outcomes are the starting point). Backwards design is a current educational trend and its applicability to second language education is often unquestioned. This becomes especially problematic when assessments get turned into grades.

On the other hand, forward procedure takes a process-oriented perspective. Then, the focus is on student actions during the activity (e.g., effort, creativity, stays on task, helps others, asks for clarification, etc.). The learning of new content can be reframed as one measure of student effort (which may benefit the shier, less vocal students). Students should be involved in the process, e.g., self-evaluations. If grades must be issued, then action-based grading may be the fairest way to do it. Second language educators have something to learn from best grading practices of those subjects where it is more commonly accepted that abilities will vary (e.g., art, music, physical education). Of course, basing grades on actions and engagement will be influenced by the degree of interest and level-appropriateness of the activities. Don't expect high levels of engagement if the activity is boring and the language incomprehensible. This exemplifies how a change in one component of the program depends on changes made to the other components.

To this point, proficiency-based assessments have not been mentioned. This type of assessment focuses on the ability to use language, which is an improvement over grammar and vocabulary tests, but ultimately, they are still language-focused. Language ability develops as a byproduct of communication. The purpose of communication is to build relationships, learn new information, and/or be entertained. Therefore, those are also the purposes and the focus of the scoring of communicative tests. Nevertheless, proficiency-based tests are useful for making program-level decisions (e.g., placement and admission) and for evaluating programs (both within and between programs). If proficiency is going to be assessed, then the best way to do it is with global ratings (e.g., using a 1-4 scale) of overall ability or by breaking that down into ratings of fluency (in the temporal sense) and comprehensibility (how easy it is to comprehend).

The major elements of this framework for second language education are summarized in Figure 2.

Approach	Design	Procedures
PRINCIPLE Maximize comprehension during communicative events	SYLLABUS procedural	CONTENT personal information, stories, culture, subject matter, themes, etc.
	ASSESSMENTS content-based, proficiency-based	ACTIVITIES content lessons, story-based, extensive reading
	GRADING action-based	STRATEGIES interaction, collaboration (especially collaborative construction)

Figure 2. *Summary of an acquisition-centered framework of second language education*

This approach is principled and process-oriented. It was all decided by starting with the study of second language acquisition (SLA) and answering how languages are acquired. The decision to focus on the acquisition of a mental grammar led to one overarching principle, i.e., maximize comprehension during communicative events. The next step was to determine what processes teachers and students should engage in to actualize this principle and to create optimal conditions for acquisition. The last step was to choose the type of syllabus and the types of assessments that would support and encourage the desired classroom procedures. This process of program development is depicted in Figure 3.

SLA -> Approach -> Procedures -> Syllabus & Assessments

Figure 3. *A principled and process-oriented approach to program development*

I would like to point out how this framework is both student-centered and teacher-centered. The curriculum is personalized, creates optimal conditions for acquisition, and expectations are developmentally appropriate. In my view, that is the definition of student-centered. It is teacher-centered, because it is predicated on trust in and support of teachers. It gives teachers considerable agency over the curriculum, which also ought to increase the teacher's investment in the program's success. This should in turn encourage teachers to reflect on their practices and seek to improve and learn more.

As was true of the approach, the features of the design and procedures of this framework are not new. But their implementation is relatively uncommon. A minority of language teachers have adopted similar principles and practices. This is essentially the framework that I adopted for five years when I worked in teaching positions that

193

allowed me the freedom to pursue acquisition-centered practices. The reason this framework has not seen wide-scale adoption is not because it is impractical or because it is incompatible with a school setting. Nonetheless, this approach is a paradigm shift and, as such, it necessitates some radical changes to the status quo.

The most fundamental change that needs to happen is in beliefs about how languages are learned. Otherwise, the rhetoric changes without a comparable change in what teachers and students do in the classroom. The success of the entire endeavor depends on teacher education and training. Surely, it is not radical to suggest that the educational system support the education and development of its teachers. With more education in SLA and exposure to a different pedagogical framework, more teachers will discard rule-based instruction as a way of developing communicative ability and instead center their practices on the acquisition of a mental grammar.

The next step after working through this book (if you have not already begun to do so) is to get experience as a student, observer, and a teacher of a comprehension-based and communicative approach. To get started as an observer, below are links to videos I recorded of my classes engaged in various activities. Check out the oral proficiency assessments to see the communicative ability that develops from this approach.

View classroom activities here:
https://www.youtube.com/playlist?list=PL8JqpkCp61R4 zRltQHINdM-Mhl5b4gZhZ

View oral assessments here:
https://www.youtube.com/playlist?list=PL8JqpkCp61R6 _C-qi-kczaFVLtF8bT9M6

References

American Council on the Teaching of Foreign Languages. (n.d.). Teach grammar as concepts in meaningful contexts in language learning. Retrieved from https://www.actfl.org/guiding-principles/teach-grammar-concepts-meaningful- contexts-language-learning

American Council on the Teaching of Foreign Languages. (2018). ACTFL OPI tester certification information packet. Retrieved from https://www.actfl.org/sites/default/files/assessments/ACTFL%20OPI%20Tester%20Certification%20Packet%202018.pdf

Anderson, J. R. (1976). *Language, Memory, and Thought*. Hillsdale, NJ: Erlbaum.

Anthony, E. M. (1963). Approach, method and technique. *English Language Teaching, 17*(2), 63–67.

Asher, J. J. (1981). Comprehension training: The evidence from laboratory and classroom studies. In H. Winitz (Eds.), *The comprehension approach to foreign language instruction* (pp. 187-222). Rowley, MA: Newbury House.

Bailey, N., Madden, C., & Krashen, S. D. (1974). Is there a "natural sequence" in adult second language learning? *Language Learning, 24*(2), 235–243.

Berko, J. (1958). The child's learning of English morphology. *Word, 14*(2-3), 150-177.

Bley-Vroman, R. (1990). The logical problem of foreign language learning. *Linguistic Analysis, 20*(1-2), 3–49.

Breen, M. P. (1984). Process syllabuses for the language classroom. In C. J. Brumfit (Eds.), *General English syllabus design* (pp. 47–60). Oxford, England: Pergamon.

Brown, J. D. (1996). *Testing in language programs*. Upper Saddle River, NJ: Prentice Hall.

Brown, R. (1973). *A first language: The early stages.* Cambridge, MA: Harvard University Press.

Brown, R. & Hanlon, C. (1970). Derivational complexity and order of acquisition in child speech. In J. R. Hayes (Eds.), *Cognition and the development of language* (pp. 11-54). New York, NY: Wiley.

Byrne, D. (1976). *Teaching oral English*. Harlow, England: Longman.

Canale, M. (1983). From communicative competence to communicative language pedagogy. In J. C. Richards & R. W. Schmidt (Eds.), *Language and communication* (pp. 2-27). London, England: Longman.

Canale, M., & Swain, M. (1980). Theoretical bases of communicative approaches to second language teaching and testing. *Applied Linguistics, 1*(1), 1-47.

Carnie, A. (2013). *Syntax: A generative introduction* (3rd ed.). Malden, MA: Wiley-Blackwell.

Carver, R. P. (1994). Percentage of unknown vocabulary words in text as a function of the relative difficulty of the text: Implications for instruction. *Journal of Reading Behavior, 26*(4), 413-437.

Center for Applied Second Language Studies. (2010). *How many hours of instruction do students need to reach intermediate-high proficiency?* Retrieved from https://casls.uoregon.edu/wp-content/uploads/pdfs/tenquestions/TBQHoursToReachIH.pdf

Center for Applied Second Language Studies. (2011). *How do proficiency levels compare between K-12 and university students?* Retrieved from https://casls.uoregon.edu/wp-content/uploads/pdfs/tenquestions/TBQLevelofLanguage.pdf

Ceo-DiFrancesco, D. (2013). Instructor target language use in today's world language classrooms. In S. Dhonau (Eds.), *Multitasks, multiskills, multiconnections: Selected papers from the 2013 central states conference on the teaching of foreign languages* (pp. 1-20). Richmond, VA: Robert M. Terry.

Chomsky, N. (1957). *Syntactic structures.* The Hague: Mouton.

Chomsky, N. (1959). [Review of the book *Verbal behavior*, by B. F. Skinner]. *Language, 35*(1), 26–58.

Chomsky, N. (1965). *Aspects of the Theory of Syntax.* Cambridge, MA: MIT Press.

Chomsky, N. (1981). *Lectures on government and binding.* Dordrecht: Foris.

Chomsky, N. (1995). *The minimalist program.* Cambridge, MA: MIT Press.

Chomsky, N. (2000). *New horizons in the study of language and mind.* Cambridge, England: Cambridge University Press.

Clarke, D. F. (1991). The negotiated syllabus: What is it and how is it likely to work? *Applied Linguistics, 12*(1), 13-28.

Comenius, J. A. (1657). *Didactica magna.* In M. W. Keatinge. (Trans., Eds.). (1907). *The great didactic of John Amos Comenius.* Vol. 2. London, England: Adam and Charles Black.

Collentine, J. (2010). The acquisition and teaching of the Spanish subjunctive: An update on current findings. *Hispania, 93*(1), 39-51.

Cook, G. (1997). Language play, language learning. *ELT Journal, 51*(3), 224–231.

Corder, S. P. (1967). The significance of learner's errors. *International Review of Applied Linguistics in Language Teaching, 5*(4), 161-170.

Davies, M. (2006). *A frequency dictionary of Spanish: Core vocabulary for learners.* New York, NY: Routledge.

Davies, M., & Face, T. L. (2006). Vocabulary coverage in Spanish textbooks: How representative is it? In N. Sagarra & A. J. Toribio (Eds.), *Selected proceedings of the 9th Hispanic Linguistics Symposium* (pp. 132–143). Somerville, MA: Cascadilla Proceedings Project.

Day, R. R. and Bamford, J. (1998). *Extensive reading in the second language classroom.* Cambridge, England: Cambridge University Press.

Day, R. R., & Bamford, J. (2002). Top ten principles for teaching extensive reading. *Reading in a Foreign Language, 14*(2), 136–141.

DeKeyser, R. M. (1994). How implicit can adult second language learning be? *AILA Review, 11*, 83-96.

DeKeyser, R. M. (1997). Beyond explicit rule learning: Automatizing second language morphosyntax. *Studies in Second Language Acquisition, 19*(2), 195-221.

DeKeyser, R. (2010). Practice for second language learning: Don't throw out the baby with the bathwater. *International Journal of English Studies, 10*(1), 155-165.

DeKeyser, R. (2015). Skill acquisition theory. In B. VanPatten & J. Williams (Eds.), *Theories in second language acquisition: An introduction* (2nd ed., pp. 94-112). New York, NY: Routledge.

Derwing, T. M., & Munro, M. J. (2009). Putting accent in its place: Rethinking obstacles to communication. *Language Teaching, 42*(4), 476-490.

de Villiers, J. G., & de Villiers, P. A. (1973). A cross-sectional study of the acquisition of grammatical morphemes in child speech. *Journal of Psycholinguistic Research, 2*(3), 267–278.

Donato, R., & Adair-Hauck, B. (1994). *PACE: A model to focus on form.* Paper presented at the annual meeting of the American Council on the Teaching of Foreign Languages, San Antonio, TX.

Dörnyei, Z. and Ottó, I. (1998). Motivation in action: A process model of L2 motivation. *Working Papers in Applied Linguistics* (Thames Valley University, London), *4,* 43–69.

Doughty, C. J. (2004). Effects of instruction on learning a second language: A critique of instructed SLA research. In B. VanPatten, J. Williams, S. Rott, & M. Overstreet (Eds.), *Form-meaning connections in second language acquisition* (pp. 181-202). Mahwah, NJ: Lawrence Erlbaum Associates.

Doughty, C. & Williams, J. (1998). Issues and terminology. In C. Doughty & J. Williams (Eds.), *Focus on form in classroom second language acquisition.* (pp. 1-11). New York, NY: Cambridge University Press.

Dulay, H. C., & Burt, M. K. (1973). Should we teach children syntax? *Language Learning, 23*(2), 245-258.

Dulay, H. C., & Burt, M. K. (1974a). Errors and strategies in child second language acquisition. *TESOL Quarterly, 8*(2), 129-136.

Dulay, H. C., & Burt, M. K. (1974b). Natural sequences in child second language acquisition. *Language Learning, 24*(1), 37-53.

Dulay, H. C. & Burt, M. K. (1974c). You can't learn without goofing: An analysis of children's second language 'errors'. In J. C. Richards (Eds.), *Error analysis: Perspectives on second language acquisition* (pp. 95-123). London, England: Longman.

Elley, W. B. & Mangubhai, F. (1983). The impact of reading on second language learning. *Reading Research Quarterly, 19*(1), 53-67.

Ellis, N. C. (2002). Frequency effects in language processing: A review with implications for theories of implicit and explicit language acquisition. *Studies in Second Language Acquisition, 24*(2), 143-188.

Ellis, N. C. (2009). Optimizing the input: Frequency and sampling in usage-based and form-focused learning. In M. H. Long & C. J. Doughty (Eds.), *The handbook of language teaching* (pp. 139-158). Oxford, England: Blackwell.

Ellis, N. C., & Wulff, S. (2015). Usage-based approaches to SLA. In B. VanPatten & J. Williams (Eds.), *Theories in second language acquisition: An introduction* (2nd ed., pp. 75-93). New York, NY: Routledge.

Ellis, R. (1984). *Classroom second language development: A Study of Classroom Interaction and Language Acquisition.* Oxford, England: Pergamon.

Ellis, R. (1989). Are classroom and naturalistic acquisition the same?: A study of the classroom acquisition of German word order rules. *Studies in Second Language Acquisition, 11*(3), 305-328.

Fathman, A. (1975). Language background, age, and the order of acquisition of English structures. In M. Burt & H. Dulay (Eds.), *On TESOL '75: New directions in second language learning, teaching and bilingual education* (pp. 33–43). Washington, DC: TESOL.

Felix, S. W. (1984). Maturational aspects of Universal Grammar. In A. Davies, C. Criper, & A. P. R. Howatt (Eds.), *Interlanguage* (pp. 133-161). Edinburgh, Scotland: Edinburgh University Press.

Felix, S. W. (1985). More evidence on competing cognitive systems. *Second Language Research, 1*(1), 47-72.

Ferris, D. (1999). The case for grammar correction in L2 writing classes: A response to Truscott (1996). *Journal of Second Language Writing, 8*(1), 1-11.

Firth, A., & Wagner, J. (1997). On discourse, communication, and (some) fundamental concepts in SLA research. *The Modern Language Journal, 81*(3), 285-300.

Frawley, W., & Lantolf, J. P. (1985). Second language discourse: A Vygotskyan perspective. *Applied Linguistics, 6*(1), 19-44.

Fullan, M. G. (1992). *Successful school improvement: The implementation perspective and beyond.* Philadelphia, PA: Open University Press.

Fullan, M. (1993). *Change forces: Probing the depths of educational reform.* London, England: The Falmer Press.

Fitzpatrick, E. A. (1933). *St. Ignatius and the Ratio studiorum.* New York, NY: McGraw-Hill.

Gardner, R. C. and Lambert, W. E. (1972). *Attitudes and motivation in second language learning.* Rowley, MA: Newbury House.

Gary, J. O., & Gary, N. (1981). Comprehension-based language instruction: Theory. In H. Winitz (Eds.), *Native language and foreign language acquisition: Annals of the New York Academy of Science* (Vol. 379, pp. 332-342).

Gass, S. M. (2017). *Input, interaction, and the second language learner.* New York, NY: Routledge.

Geeslin, K. L., & Gudmestad, A. (2010). An exploration of the range and frequency of occurrence of forms in potentially variable structures in second-language Spanish. *Studies in Second Language Acquisition, 32*(3), 433-463.

Gil, K.-H., Marsden, H., & Whong, M. (2019). The meaning of negation in the second language classroom: Evidence from 'any'. *Language Teaching Research, 23*(2), 218-236.

Gilmore, A. (2007). Authentic materials and authenticity in foreign language learning. *Language Teaching, 40*(2), 97-118.

Glisan, E. W., & Donato, R. (2017). *Enacting the Work of Language Instruction: High-Leverage Teaching Practices*. Alexandria, VA: American Council on the Teaching of Foreign Languages.

Godev, C. B. (2009). Word-frequency and vocabulary acquisition: An analysis of elementary Spanish college textbooks in the USA. *Revista de Lingüística Teórica y Aplicada, 47*(2), 51-68.

Gregg, K. R. (1984). Krashen's monitor and Occam's razor. *Applied Linguistics, 5*(2), 79-100.

Gregg, K. R. (1996). The logical and developmental problems of second language acquisition. In W. C. Ritchie & T. K. Bhatia (Eds.), *Handbook of second language acquisition* (pp. 49-81). San Diego, CA: Academic Press.

Gregg, K. R. (1997). UG and SLA theory: The story so far. *Revista Canaria de Estudios Ingleses, 34*, 69-99.

Gregg, K. R. (2003). SLA theory: Construction and assessment. In M. H. Long & C. J. Doughty (Eds.), *The handbook of second language acquisition* (pp. 831-865). Oxford, England: Blackwell.

Guarini, B. (1958). *De ordine docendi et discendi.* In E. Garin (D. Musumeci, Trans., Eds.). *Il pensiero pedagogico dello Umanesimo.* (pp. 434-471). Florence: Giuntine and Sansoni.

Guarini, G. (1958). *Le epistole di Guarini da Verona.* In E. Garin (D. Musumeci, Trans., Eds.). *Il pensiero pedagogico dello Umanesimo.* (pp. 306-433). Florence: Giuntine and Sansoni.

Harley, B. (1989). Functional grammar in French immersion: A classroom Experiment. *Applied Linguistics, 10*(3), 331-360.

Harley, B., & Swain, M. (1984). The interlanguage of immersion students and its implications for second language teaching. In A. Davies, C. Criper, & A. P. R. Howatt (Eds.), *Interlanguage* (pp. 291-311). Edinburgh: Edinburgh University Press.

Hastings, A. J. (1995). The FOCAL SKILLS approach: an assessment. In F. R. Eckman, D. Highland, P. W. Lee, J. Mileham, & R. R. Weber (Eds.), *Second language acquisition: Theory and pedagogy* (pp. 29-44). Malwah, N.J.: Lawrence Erlbaum Associates.

Hastings, A. (2003). The FOCAL SKILLS Advantage. Retrieved from https://web.archive.org/web/20170907112049/http://www.focalskills.info:80/articles/fsadvantage.html

Herman, E. (2017). *Assessing proficiency in the classroom.* Scotts Valley, CA: CreateSpace Independent Publishing Platform.

Higgs, T. V., & Clifford, R. (1982). The push toward communication. In T. V. Higgs (Eds.), *Curriculum, competence, and the foreign language teacher* (pp. 57–79). Stokie, IL: National Textbook.

Hornstein, N., & Lightfoot, D. (1981). *Explanation in linguistics. The logical problem of language acquisition.* London, England: Longman.

Huberman, M. (1992). Critical introduction. In M. G. Fullan (Eds.), *Successful school improvement: The implementation perspective and beyond* (pp. 1-20). Philadelphia, PA: Open University Press.

Hymes, D. (1972). On communicative competence. In J. Pride & J. Holmes (Eds.), *Sociolinguistics* (pp. 269–93). Harmondsworth, London: Penguin Books.

Jackendoff, R. (2002). *Foundations of language: Brain, meaning, grammar, evolution.* Oxford, England: Oxford University Press.

Jeon, E.-Y. & Day, R. R. (2016). The effectiveness of ER on reading proficiency: A meta-analysis. *Reading in a Foreign Language, 28*(2), 246-265.

Jones, R. L., & Tschirner, E. (2006). *A frequency dictionary of German: Core vocabulary for learners.* New York, NY: Routledge.

Kellerman, E. (1985). If at first you do succeed. . . In S. Gass and C. Madden (Eds.), *Input in second language acquisition* (pp. 345-353). Rowley, MA: Newbury House.

Kintsch, W. (1998). *Comprehension: A paradigm for cognition.* New York, NY: Cambridge University Press.

Kintsch, W., & Kintsch, E. (2005). Comprehension. In S. G. Paris & S. A. Stahl (Eds.), *Children's reading comprehension and assessment* (pp. 71–92). Mahwah, NJ: Erlbaum.

Kintsch, W., & Rawson, K. (2005). Comprehension. In M. Snowling & C. Hulme (Eds.), *The science of reading: A handbook* (pp. 209-226). Malden, MA: Blackwell.

Kintsch, W., & van Dijk, T. (1978). Toward a model of text comprehension and production. *Psychological Review, 85*(5), 363-394.

Krashen, S. D. (1975, December). *A model of adult second language performance*. Paper presented at the Linguistic Society of America, San Francisco, CA.

Krashen, S. D. (1976). Formal and informal linguistic environments in language acquisition and language learning. *TESOL Quarterly, 10*(2), 157-168.

Krashen, S. D. (1977). The monitor model for adult second language performance. In M. Burt, H. Dulay, & M. Finocchiaro (Eds.), *Viewpoints on English as a second language* (pp. 213-221). New York, NY: Regents.

Krashen, S. D. (1981). The "fundamental pedagogical principle" in second language teaching. *Studia Linguistica, 35*(1-2), 50-70.

Krashen, S. D. (1982). *Principles and practice in second language acquisition*. New York, NY: Pergamon Press.

Krashen, S. (1989). We acquire vocabulary and spelling by reading: Additional evidence for the input hypothesis. *The Modern Language Journal, 73*(4), 440-464.

Krashen, S. (1998). Comprehensible output? *System, 26*(2), 175-182.

Krashen, S. D. (2003). Current issues and controversies: Does grammar teaching work? What about 'comprehensible output'? In S. D. Krashen (Eds.), *Explorations in language acquisition and use* (pp. 30-67). Portsmouth, NH: Heinemann.

Krashen, S. D. (2004). *The power of reading: Insights from the research* (2nd ed.). Portsmouth, NH: Hienemann.

Krashen, S. D. & Terrell, T. D. (1983). *The natural approach: Language acquisition in the classroom.* Hayward, CA: Alemany Press.

Kroll, J. F., & Stewart, E. (1994). Category interference in translation and picture naming: Evidence for asymmetric connections between bilingual memory representations. *Journal of Memory and Language, 33*(2), 149–174.

Kumaravadivelu, B. (1994). The postmethod condition: (E)merging strategies for second/foreign language teaching. *TESOL Quarterly, 28*(1), 27-48.

Labov, W. (1972). *Sociolinguistic patterns.* Philadelphia, PA: University of Pennsylvania Press.

Lantolf, J. P. (2011). The sociocultural approach to second language acquisition: Sociocultural theory, second language acquisition, and artificial L2 development. In D. Atkinson (Ed.), *Alternative approaches to second language acquisition,* (pp. 24-47). New York, NY: Routledge.

Lantolf, J. P., Thorne, S. L., & Poehner, M. E. (2015). Sociocultural theory and second language development. In B. VanPatten & J. Williams (Eds.), *Theories in second language acquisition: An introduction* (2nd ed., pp. 207-226). New York, NY: Routledge.

Larsen-Freeman, D., & Long, M. H. (1991). *An introduction to second language acquisition research.* London, England: Longman.

Lee, J., Jang, J., & Plonsky, L. (2015). The effectiveness of second language pronunciation instruction: A meta-analysis. *Applied Linguistics, 36*(3), 345-366.

Lee, J. F., & VanPatten, B. (2003). *Making communicative language teaching happen* (2nd ed.). New York, NY: McGraw-Hill.

Lightbown, P. (1983). Exploring relationships between developmental and instructional sequences in L2 acquisition. In H. Seliger and M. H. Long (Eds.), *Classroom oriented research in second language acquisition* (pp. 217–243). Rowley, MA: Newbury House.

Lightbown, P. M. (1985). Great expectations: Second-language acquisition research and classroom teaching. *Applied Linguistics, 6*(2), 173-189.

Lightbown, P. M. (2000). Anniversary article: Classroom SLA research and second language teaching. *Applied Linguistics, 21*(4), 431-462.

Lightbown, P. M., & Spada, N. (2013). Second language learning. In P. M. Lightbown & N. Spada (Eds.), *How languages are learned* (4th ed., pp. 35-74). Oxford, England: Oxford University Press.

Lipinski, S. (2010). A frequency analysis of vocabulary in three first-year textbooks of German. *Die Unterrichtspraxis/Teaching German, 43*(2), 167-174.

Long, M. (1981). Input, interaction, and second language acquisition. In H. Winitz (Eds.), *Native language and foreign language acquisition: Annals of the New York Academy of Science* (Vol. 379, pp. 259–278).

Long, M. H. (1991). Focus on form: A design feature in language teaching methodology. In K. de Bot, R. B. Ginsberg, & C. Kramsch (Eds.), *Foreign language research in cross-cultural perspective* (pp. 39–52). Amsterdam: John Benjamins.

Long, M. H. (2000). Focus on form in task-based language teaching. In R. L. Lambert & E. Shohamy (Eds.), *Language policy and pedagogy* (pp. 179–92). Philadelphia, PA: John Benjamins.

Long, M. H. (2009). Methodological principles for language teaching. In M. H. Long & C. J. Doughty (Eds.), *The handbook of language teaching* (pp. 373-394). Oxford, England: Blackwell.

Long, M. H. & Sato, C. J. (1983). Classroom foreigner talk discourse: Forms and functions of teachers' questions. In M. Long & H. Seliger (Eds.), *Classroom oriented research in second language acquisition* (pp. 268-286). Rowley, MA: Newbury House.

Lonsdale, C. (2006). *The third ear: You can learn any language.* Hong Kong: Third Ear Books.

Loyola, I. (1954). The constitutions of the Society of Jesus. Part IV. In G. E. Ganss. (Trans., Eds.). *Saint Ignatius' idea of a Jesuit university* (pp. 271-335). Milwaukee: The Marquette University Press.

Marsden, H., & Slabakova, R. (2019). Grammatical meaning and the second language classroom: Introduction. *Language Teaching Research, 23*(2), 147-157.

McLaughlin, B. (1978). The monitor model: Some methodological considerations. *Language Learning, 28*(2), 309-332.

McNeill, D. (1966). Developmental psycholinguistics. In F. Smith & G. A. Miller (Eds.), *The genesis of language: A psycholinguistic approach.* Cambridge, MA: MIT Press.

Mitchell, R., & Myles, F. (2004). *Second language learning theories* (2nd ed.). London, England: Hodder Arnold.

Mitchell, R., Myles, F., & Marsden, E. (2013). *Second language learning theories* (3rd ed.). New York, NY: Routledge.

Morgan-Short, K., Finger, I., Grey, S., & Ullman, M.T. (2012). Second language processing shows increased native-like neural responses after months of no exposure. *PLoS ONE, 7*(3): e32974.

Morrow, K. (1977). Authentic texts and ESP. In Holden, S. (Eds.), *English for specific purposes* (pp. 13-17). London, England: Modern English Publications.

Murphy, B., & Hastings, A. (2006). The utter hopelessness of explicit grammar teaching. *The International Journal of Foreign Language Teaching, 2*(2), 9-11.

Musumeci, D. (1997). *Breaking tradition: An exploration of the historical relationship between theory and practice in second language teaching.* New York, NY: McGraw-Hill.

Musumeci, D. (2009). History of Language Teaching. In M. H. Long & C. J. Doughty (Eds.), *The handbook of language teaching* (pp. 42-62). Oxford, England: Blackwell.

Nation, I. S. P. (2006). How large a vocabulary is needed for reading and listening? *The Canadian Modern Language Review, 63*(1), 59-82.

Nation, I. S. P. (2013). *Learning vocabulary in another language* (2nd ed.). New York, NY: Cambridge University Press.

Nation, I. S. P. (2016). Response to Tom Cobb. *Reading in a Foreign Language, 28*(2), 305-306.

Nord, J. R. (1981). Three steps leading to listening fluency: A beginning. In H. Winitz (Eds.), *The comprehension approach to foreign language instruction* (pp. 69-100). Rowley, MA: Newbury House.

Norris, J., & Ortega, L. (2000). Effectiveness of L2 instruction: A research synthesis and quantitative meta-analysis. *Language Learning, 50*(3), 417-528.

Paulston, C. B. (1970). Structural pattern drills: A classification. *Foreign Language Annals, 4*(2), 187-193.

Pérez-Leroux, A. T., & Glass, W. R. (1999). Null anaphora in Spanish second language acquisition: Probabilistic versus generative approaches. *Second Language Research, 15*(2), 220–249.

Pica, T. (1983). Adult acquisition of English as a second language under different conditions of exposure. *Language Learning, 33*(4), 465–497.

Pica, T., Young, R., & Doughty, C. (1987). The impact of interaction on comprehension. *TESOL Quarterly 21*(4), 737-758.

Pienemann, M. (1998). *Language processing and second language development: Processability Theory.* Amsterdam, Netherlands: John Benjamins.

Pienemann, M. (2005). *Cross-linguistic aspects of Processability Theory.* Amsterdam, Netherlands: John Benjamins.

Pienemann, M. (2011). Developmental schedules. In M. Pienemann & J. U. Kessler (Eds.), *Studying processability theory: An introductory textbook* (Vol. 1, pp. 3-11). Philadelphia, PA: John Benjamins.

Pinker, S. (1994). *The language instinct: How the mind creates language.* New York, NY: Harper Perennial.

Prabhu, N. S. (1987). *Second language pedagogy.* Oxford, England: Oxford University Press.

Ray, B. & Seely, C. (2019). *Fluency through TPR Storytelling: Achieving real language acquisition in school* (Revised 8th ed.). Berkeley, CA: Command Performance Language Institute.

Richards, J. C. (2013). Curriculum approaches in language teaching: Forward, central, and backward design. *RELC Journal, 44*(1), 5-33.

Richards, J. C., & Rodgers, T. S. (2014). The nature of approaches and methods in language teaching. In J. C. Richards & T. S. Rodgers (Eds.), *Approaches and methods in language teaching* (3rd ed., pp. 20-43). Cambridge, England: Cambridge University Press.

Rothman, J. (2008). Aspect selection in adult L2 Spanish and the Competing Systems Hypothesis: When pedagogical and linguistic rules conflict. *Languages in Contrast, 8*(1), 74-106.

Rothman, J., & Slabakova, R. (2018). The generative approach to SLA and its place in modern second language studies. *Studies in Second Language Acquisition, 40*(2), 417-442.

Sandrock, P., Swender, E., Cowles, M. A., Martin, C., & Vicars, R. (2012). *ACTFL performance descriptors for language learners.* Alexandria, VA: American Council on the Teaching of Foreign Languages.

Savignon, S. J. (1972). *Communicative competence: An experiment in foreign language teaching.* Philadelphia, PA: Center for Curriculum Development.

Savignon, S. J. (1976, April 23). *Communicative competence: Theory and classroom practice.* Paper presented at the Central States Conference on the Teaching of Foreign Languages, Detroit, MI.

Savignon, S. J. (1997). *Communicative competence theory and classroom practice: Texts and contexts in second language learning* (2nd ed.). New York, NY: McGraw-Hill.

Savignon, S. J. (2017, March 7). Communicative competence. In J. I. Liontas (Eds.), *The TESOL encyclopedia of English language teaching* (pp. 1– 7). Hoboken, NJ: Wiley. Retrieved from https://doi.org/10.1002/9781118784235.eelt0047

Schmidt, R. W. (1990). The role of consciousness in second language learning. *Applied Linguistics, 11*(2), 129-158.

Schmitt, N., Jiang, X., & Grabe, W. (2011). The percentage of words known in a text and reading comprehension. *The Modern Language Journal, 95*(1), 26–43.

Schmitt, N., & Schmitt, D. (2014). A reassessment of frequency and vocabulary size in L2 vocabulary teaching. *Language Teaching, 47*(4), 484-503.

Schwartz, B. D. (1990). Un-motivating the motivation for the fundamental difference hypothesis. In H. Burmeister & P. Rounds (Eds.), *Variability in second language acquisition* (pp. 667–684). Eugene, OR: University of Oregon.

Schwartz, B. D. (1993). On explicit and negative data effecting and affecting competence and linguistic behavior. *Studies in Second Language Acquisition, 15*(2), 147-163.

Schwartz, B. D. & Sprouse, R. A. (2013). Generative approaches and the poverty of the stimulus. In J. Herschensohn & M. Young-Scholten (Eds.), *The Cambridge handbook of second language acquisition* (pp. 137-158). Cambridge, England: Cambridge University Press.

Selinker, L. (1972). Interlanguage. *International Review of Applied Linguistics in Language Teaching, 10*(3), 209–230.

Semke, H. D. (1984). Effects of the red pen. *Foreign Language Annals, 17*(3), 195-202.

Sharwood Smith, M. (1993). Input enhancement in instructed SLA: Theoretical bases. *Studies in Second Language Acquisition, 15*(2), 165–179.

Sharwood Smith, M. (2004). In two minds about grammar: On the interaction of linguistic and metalinguistic knowledge in performance. *Transactions of the Philological Society, 102*(2), 255–280.

Sharwood Smith, M. (2019). About the MCF and MOGUL. Retrieved from http://mogulframe.co.uk/aims-scope-2

Sharwood Smith, M., & Truscott, J. (2005). Stages or continua in second language acquisition: A MOGUL solution. *Applied Linguistics, 26*(2), 219–240.

Sharwood Smith, M., & Truscott, J. (2014a). Explaining input enhancement: A MOGUL perspective. *International Review of Applied Linguistics in Language Teaching, 52*(3), 253-281.

Sharwood Smith, M., & Truscott, J. (2014b). *The multilingual mind: A modular processing perspective.* New York, NY: Cambridge University Press.

Shehadeh, A. (2002). Comprehensible output, from occurrence to acquisition: An agenda for acquisitional research. *Language Learning, 52*(3), 597-647.

Shrum, J. L., & Glisan, E. W. (2016). *Teacher's handbook: Contextualized language instruction* (5th ed.). Boston, MA: Cengage Learning.

Spada, N., & Tomita, Y. (2010). Interactions between type of instruction and type of language feature: A meta-analysis. *Language Learning, 60*(2), 263-308.

Swain, M. (1984). Large-scale communicative language testing: A case study. In S. J. Savignon & M. S. Berns (Eds.), *Initiatives in communicative language teaching* (pp. 185-201). Reading, MA: Addison-Wesley.

Swain, M. (1985). Communicative competence: Some roles of comprehensible input and comprehensible output in its development. In S. Gass, and C. Madden (Eds.), *Input in second language acquisition* (pp. 235-253). Rowley, MA: Newbury House.

Swain, M. (1995). Three functions of output in second language learning. In G. Cook & B. Seidlhofer (Eds.), *Principle and practice in applied linguistics: Studies in honour of H. G. Widdowson* (pp. 125–144). Oxford, England: Oxford University Press.

Swain, M. (2000). The output hypothesis and beyond: Mediating acquisition through collaborative dialogue. In J. Lantolf (Eds.), *Sociocultural approaches to second language research* (pp. 97–114). Oxford, England: Oxford University Press.

Swain, M. (2006). Language, agency, and collaboration in advanced language proficiency. In H. Byrnes (Eds.), *Advanced language learning: The contribution of Halliday and Vygotsky* (pp. 95–108). London, England: Continuum.

Swain, M., & Lapkin, S. (1995). Problems in output and the cognitive processes they generate: A step towards second language learning. *Applied Linguistics, 16*(3), 371-391.

Swender, E., Conrad, D. J., & Vicars, R. (2012). *ACTFL proficiency guidelines 2012.* Alexandria, VA: American Council on the Teaching of Foreign Languages.

TEDx. (2013, November 20). *Chris Lonsdale: How to learn any language in six months* [Video file]. Retrieved from https://youtu.be/d0yGdNEWdn0

Terrell, T. D. (1977). A natural approach to second language acquisition and learning. *Modern Language Journal, 61*(7), 325-336.

Terrell, T. D., Baycroft, B., & Perrone, C. (1987). The subjunctive in Spanish interlanguage: Accuracy and comprehensibility. In B. VanPatten, T. R. Dvorak, & J. F. Lee (Eds.), *Foreign language learning: A research perspective* (pp. 19-32). Cambridge, MA: Newbury House.

Teschner, R. V. (1987). A profile of the specialization and expertise of lower division foreign language program directors in American universities. *The Modern Language Journal, 71*(1), 28-35.

Toth, P. D., & Davin, K. J. (2016). The sociocognitive imperative of L2 pedagogy. *The Modern Language Journal, 100*(Suppl.), 148-168.

Truscott, J. (1996). The case against grammar correction in L2 writing classes. *Language Learning, 46*(2), 327–369.

Truscott, J. (1998). Noticing in second language acquisition: A critical review. *Second Language Research, 14*(2), 103–35.

Truscott, J. (1999). The case for "The case against grammar correction in L2 writing classes": A response to Ferris. *Journal of Second Language Writing, 8*(2), 111-122.

Truscott, J., & Sharwood Smith, M. (2004). Acquisition by processing: A modular approach to language development. *Bilingualism: Language and Cognition, 7*(1), 1– 20.

Truscott, J., & Sharwood Smith, M. (2011). Input, intake, and consciousness: The quest for a theoretical foundation. *Studies in Second Language Acquisition, 33*(4), 497–528.

Ullman, M. T. (2015). The declarative/procedural model: A neurobiologically motivated theory of first and second language. In B. VanPatten & J. Williams (Eds.), *Theories in second language acquisition: An introduction* (2nd ed., pp. 135–158). New York, NY: Routledge.

Van den Branden, K. (2007). Second language education: Practice in perfect learning conditions? In R. M. DeKeyser (Eds.), *Practice in a second language: Perspectives from applied linguistics and cognitive psychology* (pp. 161-179). Cambridge, England: Cambridge University Press.

VanPatten, B. (1986). Second language acquisition research and the learning/teaching of Spanish: Some research findings and implications. *Hispania, 69*(1), 202-216.

VanPatten, B. (1988). How juries get hung: Problems with the evidence for a focus on form in teaching. *Language Learning, 38*(2), 243-260.

VanPatten, B. (1994). Evaluating the role of consciousness in second language acquisition: Terms, linguistic features & research methodology. *AILA Review, 11,* 27–36.

VanPatten, B. (1996). *Input processing and grammar instruction.* Norwood, NJ: Ablex.

VanPatten, B. (1998). Perceptions of and perspectives on the term "communicative." *Hispania, 81*(4), 925-932.

VanPatten, B. (2004). Input processing in second language acquisition. In B. VanPatten (Eds.), *Processing instruction: Theory, research, and commentary* (pp. 5–31). Mahwah, NJ: Lawrence Erlbaum Associates.

VanPatten, B. (2015a). Foundations of processing instruction. *International Review of Applied Linguistics in Language Teaching, 53*(2), 91-109.

VanPatten, B. (2015b). Input processing in adult SLA. In B. VanPatten & J. Williams (Eds.), *Theories in second language acquisition: An introduction* (2nd ed., pp. 113–134). New York, NY: Routledge.

VanPatten, B. (2015c). *Hispania* white paper: Where are the experts? *Hispania, 98*(1), 2-13.

VanPatten, B. (2017). *While we're on the topic: BVP on language, acquisition, and classroom practice.* Alexandria, VA: American Council on the Teaching of Foreign Languages.

VanPatten, B., Borst, S., Collopy, E., Qualin, A., & Price, J. (2013). Explicit information, grammatical sensitivity, and the first-noun strategy: A cross-linguistic study in processing instruction. *The Modern Language Journal, 97*(2), 506–527.

VanPatten, B., & Cadierno, T. (1993a). Explicit instruction and input processing. *Studies in Second Language Acquisition, 15*(2), 225–243.

VanPatten, B., & Cadierno, T. (1993b). Input processing and second language acquisition: A role for instruction. *The Modern Language Journal, 77*(1), 45–57.

VanPatten, B., Keating, G. D., & Leeser, M. J. (2012). Missing verbal inflections as a representational problem: Evidence from self-paced reading. *Linguistic Approaches to Bilingualism, 2*(2), 109–140.

VanPatten, B., & Oikkenon, S. (1996). Explanation versus structured input in processing instruction. *Studies in Second Language Acquisition, 18*(4), 495-510.

VanPatten, B., & Rothman, J. (2014). Against "rules." In A. Benati, C. Laval, & M. J. Arche (Eds.), *The grammar dimension in instructed second language acquisition: Theory, research, and practice* (pp. 15–35). London, England: Bloomsbury.

White, L. (1987). Against comprehensible input: The input hypothesis and the development of second-language competence. *Applied Linguistics, 8*(2), 95-110.

White, L. (1991). Adverb placement in second language acquisition: Some effects of positive and negative evidence in the classroom. *Second Language Research, 7*(2), 133-161.

White, L. (2003). *Second language acquisition and universal grammar.* Cambridge, England: Cambridge University Press.

Winitz, H., & Reeds, J. A. (1973). Rapid acquisition of a foreign language (German) by the avoidance of speaking. *International Review of Applied Linguistics in Language Teaching*, *11*(4), 295-318.

Wong, W., & VanPatten, B. (2003). The evidence is IN: Drills are OUT. *Foreign Language Annals*, *36*(3), 403-423.

Yamashita, J. (2015). In search of the nature of extensive reading in L2: Cognitive, affective, and pedagogical perspectives. *Reading in a Foreign Language*, *27*(1), 168-181.

Young, D. Y. (1990). An investigation of students' perspectives on anxiety and speaking. *Foreign Language Annals*, *23*(6), 539-553.

Yu, B. (1998). *A comparison of English proficiency gains in one FOCAL SKILLS and two traditional ESL programs* (Unpublished master's thesis), Shenandoah University, Winchester, VA.

Author Index

Subject Index

Made in the USA
San Bernardino, CA
04 May 2020

70971324R00135